faith
matters
reflections
on God

kyle c. dodd

FAITH MATTERS

Kyle Dodd

ISBN 1-929478-49-6

Cross Training Publishing
P.O. Box 1541
Grand Island, NE 68802
800-430-8588

Library of Congress Cataloging in Publication Data in Progress.

Published by Cross Training Publishing,
P.O. Box 1541
Grand Island, NE 68802
1-800-430-8588

ACKNOWLEDGEMENTS

I would like to dedicate this book to my faithful bride Sharon Elizabeth Dodd, who is my earthly rock, wise counselor, and intimate lover. To my four sons who help make up "Teamdodd": Daniel, Dustin, Drew, and Davis and teach us daily about , God's forgiveness, grace, and resilient love. Saving the best for last, to my Lord, Savior, and daddy, Jesus Christ who continues to use an old crooked stick like me despite my earthly frailties. To God be ALL the glory and honor. Finish strong!

Kyle C. Dodd

FOREWORD

Kyle is a very gifted writer and communicator who knows the REAL needs of people. You will benefit personally because his writing is a merger of the truth of Scripture applied to the issues you and I face daily.

Dennis Rainey
Executive Director of FamilyLife Ministries
in association with Campus Crusade for Christ

UNDISCIPLED DISCIPLES

Go therefore and make disciples of all nations, baptizing them in the name
of the Father, Son and Holy Spirit.
Matthew 28:19

★ ★ ★

In 1937, Dietrich Bonhoeffer used several terms in his book, *The Cost of Discipleship*, to describe our social rendition of faith in God as "easy Christianity" and "cheap grace." The word disciple is used 269 times in the New Testament while the word "Christian" is only found three times to refer to the disciples. The New Testament is written by disciples, about disciples and for disciples. Our contemporary churches today are filled with members who have not yet decided to follow Christ. The above verse has been rewritten in our western culture to read more like "make converts and baptize them into church membership." Why? Where has our alignment gotten out-of-line in our understanding of our purpose and responsibility for being a disciple and then making a disciple? A disciple is not some heavy duty model of a Christian. Discipleship was and is being with Christ and today is not something one can do through a correspondence course. The cost of not having discipleship is a lack of abiding peace. The results of discipleship are a life penetrated with love, faith that sees as God does, hope in the middle of chaos and power to do what's right!

In 1973, a guy named Aaron Fleming came to my high school to take 12 guys and disciple them through their senior year. I was fortunate to be one of those 12 guys, and today I attribute my being in full-time ministry to God and Aaron. You see . . . being a disciple who passed on his life to others cost Aaron a lot, yet true discipleship is forfeiting the things normally sought in human life for a worthy cause. The cost of discipleship is exactly that abundance of life Christ said He came to bring (John 10:10). My question to you is this . . . are you an Apostle Paul and if so, who is your Timothy? This world lacks our ultimate calling to "plant trees (disciples) that we will never sit under for shade (no hidden agendas)." Be a fisher of men (or women), cuz the fish "shore" are bitin'. So as you start the new year, remember "we are called to be fishers of men, not keepers of the aquarium."

★ ★ ★

Further Study: Read Luke 14:26-35 and discuss the cost of discipleship. Does God call the qualified for His service or does He qualify the called?

OVERCOMERS

Whoever wishes to be great among you must first be a servant.
Matthew 20:26

★ ★ ★

For years now you will find at the bottom of every letter that goes out of my office two powerful words . . . "Press On." No one exemplifies this phrase more than a guy named Doug Blevins. At the beginning of the 1997 NFL season, you found him not on a sofa with remote in hand, but on the sidelines of the Miami Dolphins at Pro Player Stadium with stopwatch in hand. Doug is the kicking coach for the Dolphins, and his knowledge of the art of punting, kicking off and field goal attempts leads one to believe he must be a retired NFL kicker himself. False. Doug was stricken with cerebral palsy at birth and is confined to a motorized wheel-chair. You might be asking yourself, "What does he know about kicking a football?" The answer: physically and experientially nothing, but mentally a lot. Physical handicaps affect your body, but not your mind and will. Doug isn't new at this; he coached in college and for the New York Jets and New England Patriots. The head coach of the Dolphins is no merciful man and hired Doug because he can help the Dolphins win games, not because he felt sorry for him.

What a tremendous story of a man who has an "iron will" to succeed despite his obvious handicap. You don't have to be crippled or mentally handicapped by your mind's limitations, sin, lack of motivation or past mistakes. In the above passage, Jesus didn't get mad at James and John for wanting to aspire to greatness; He just said to do it His way. We walk by folks every day who are disabled in one form or another, yet the power of God and their willingness to serve allow them victory over setbacks. My high school coach used to say, "Make a setback be a comeback." How true it is that all of us (you included) have the capability to do all things through Christ who fuels our tanks with that high octane (Philippians 4:13). God wants to lead us to personal victories and greatness on this planet far more than we want to follow. Look at the example Doug and so many others have set. Don't forget we also have a Savior who goes exceedingly, abundantly, beyond our every expectation (Ephesians 3:20). Go get it!

★ ★ ★

Further Study: What do you feel are your own personal handicaps or disabilities that hinder you? How can you and God overcome those?

7

FINISH WELL

Then I (Isaiah) *said, "Lord, for how long must I do this?" and the Lord said, "Until cities are devastated and without inhabitant, houses are without people and the land is utterly desolate* (until it is finished!)."
Isaiah 6:11

★ ★ ★

In our society, the employee, family, coach or youth pastor that finishes with the same intensity he/she started with is a rare breed. Now, I'm not saying that God can't call you to another occupation, but what happened to the good, old "loyalty" thing? Why is it so hard to find people sticking with a job until it's finished? People hop from job to job, spouse to spouse like a cricket on the hood of a car on a hot summer day. This scary pattern not only penetrates into marriages, but into a person's relationship with Christ. Did you know that out of all the Bible characters who started the race with a personal relationship with God, 400 in all, only 80 (1 in 5) finished well? No, I'm not saying they lost their salvation, but 320 out of 400 went astray. Why? What causes the human being to become so fickle? What did the 80 who did stick-it-out all have in common to "press on" till the end? Let's take a look at some qualities needed to finish well:

#1   All 80 were humble at heart.
#2   All 80 had an intimate relationship with God.
#3   All 80 were obedient to God's standards.
#4   All 80 had child-like faith in God.
#5   All 80 were able to receive counsel without taking offense as they grew old.

Wow! Is that interesting or what? Folks like Noah, Moses, Abraham, Sarah, Abel, Isaiah, Micah, Samuel, Paul and Jesus finished the job. I could mention others, but they wouldn't fit on this page. The real issue is . . . will you be able to add your name to this list, or are you developing a quitter's pattern today that will prevent a strong finish? "Winners never quit and quitters never win." Be the one out of five who finishes well!

★ ★ ★

Further Study: If someone were to ask whether or not you finish what you start, what would you say? Do you possess any of the five qualities it takes to finish? Why or why not?

SOLOMON SYNDROME

If any of you lacks wisdom, let him ask of God, who gives to all men generously
and without reproach, and it will be given to him. But let him ask in
faith without any doubting, for the one who doubts is like the
surf of the sea driven and tossed by the wind.
James 1:5-6

★ ★ ★

It's called "recovery time" in sporting events, but I call it "getting your clock cleaned." This devotion comes on the heels of my best effort, at the young age of 38, trying my hand at "boogie-boarding" on the beach at New Smyrna, Florida. We were there on a family vacation in early August, and I was trying to teach my oldest son, Daniel, how to ride the pipe of a breaking wave about 100 feet off-shore. This hip form of "baby boomer" surfing is harder than it looks, especially when your timing is off and your coconut (head) gets cracked by the power and weight of an 8-foot wave. The power of the surf is unbelievable, and trust me when I say it can make ya' see double if you're not careful.

In the above passage of scripture, James (half brother to Jesus) speaks from his experience as a fisherman. To be in a boat on the ocean during a storm is a bit more stressful than me on a mini-surfboard facing a 6-foot wave. The issue he deals with is wisdom. People are spouting all kinds of wisdom being used in the world today. James is speaking here of Godly wisdom, with a Divine source. King Solomon, considered the wisest man ever, got all his wisdom from God, and so can you. We all need heavenly wisdom to make it day to day. We need extra eyes to see situations from a Godly perspective. How do you get this set of spiritual eyes? The same way Solomon did; he asked God. The key number in this formula is that you must have faith (Hebrews 11:1) in God to ask. I can speak from experience that a lack of faith leads to a tumble you don't want to take. Don't doubt for one minute that God doesn't get excited with goose bumps to give you, yes you, a large dose of wisdom. Trust me . . . the ride will be a lot smoother.

★ ★ ★

Further Study: Why is wisdom important? Read Hebrews 11:1 and talk about what faith really is. Now take a minute and ask God to give you heavenly wisdom.

9

THE PLAGUE OF DISOBEDIENCE

*The locust covered the surface of the whole land so that the land was darkened;
they ate every plant and all fruit, nothing green was left through all of
Egypt. Then Pharaoh hurriedly called for Moses and Aaron.
"I have sinned against the Lord your God; please forgive
my sin and make an appeal to the Lord to
remove this death from me."*
Exodus 10:15–17

★ ★ ★

In our generation, areas having the potential for a locust outbreak are monitored by international agencies using satellite reconnaissance and other technology. The swarms of locusts are met by aircraft and trucks carrying powerful pesticides to stomp out their plague. However, if the locusts are not destroyed quickly after they hatch, control efforts are minimally effective. An example of this was in 1988 during the civil war in Chad. The fighting prevented help in attacking the hatch, and a destructive swarm spread throughout North Africa. Some of the poorest nations were devastated, and Europe was threatened. It's difficult for us in the western world to appreciate the threat of a locust plague in earlier periods of time. Locusts were the eighth plague on Egypt, and images of locusts were carved in sixth-dynasty tombs at Saggara over three-quarters of a millennium earlier. Locusts can migrate great distances and have even been observed 1,200 miles at sea. In 1889, a swarm across the Red Sea was estimated to cover 2,000 square miles, containing up to 120 million insects per square mile.

So why am I on this bug binge? To point out the severity of disobedience to God. No, I'm not saying that the next time you make a mistake God is going to send down a swarm of locusts to take up residency in your hair. I am saying there were in Old Testament times, and still are today, consequences for our actions. I know this tarnishes the "God is Love" image you may have locked in your mind, but it is the truth of Scripture and of the character of Yahweh (God). God is going to bless us when we obey Him or judge us with consequences when we don't. No, no, no . . . we are not talking about a perfect Christian here, just one who "presses on" towards being as much like Christ as possible. Through God's grace and a lot of divine help we can please our Lord.

★ ★ ★

Further Study: Why does God want you to obey Him? What was the purpose of the locust plagues or any other plagues?

YOU NEED A RITUAL

Thus says the Lord, "The fast of the fourth, the fast of the fifth, the fast of the seventh, and the fast of the tenth months will become joy, gladness, and cheerful feasts for the house of Judah; so love, truth and peace."
Zechariah 8:19

★ ★ ★

At the finals of the Compaq World Putting Championship held at Walt Disney World in Florida, the contestants had different styles, different strokes and different degrees of success. However, they all had something in common–time after time, every player made a consistent series of movements before each putt, a "ritual." The rituals were not the same. In fact, with 200 players reaching the final stage of the tournament, there were 200 different ways of settling in and setting up for a putt. All 200 contestants took this tourney seriously with a $250,000 purse going to the winner.

Other sports are not unlike golf in the sense of rituals or habits. Consider basketball players at the free-throw line, a gymnast during warm-up, pitchers on the mound, swimmers before a meet and so on. We are all creatures of habit, yet it seems we lack ritual in our spiritual lives. The purpose of a ritual in the athletic arena is to better prepare yourself for your event. We need rituals in our personal and family lives as well, like daily prayer and scripture reading, sit-down mealtimes as a family and family devotions around the table. What is your personal and family ritual? What helps you daily to compete in the game of life? Without rituals you usually find your game is off and you fail at those simple putts in life. The greatest journeys in our history began with one single step. If you have no ritual, begin today. Spiritual rituals far surpass any putting championship purse you'd ever win, and the trophies last through eternity.

★ ★ ★

Further Study: Why are rituals so important in sports? What are some of your consistent family rituals? What new rituals could you begin this week?

TRUE OR FALSE

*Do not quench the spirit; do not despise prophetic utterances. But
examine everything carefully; hold fast to that which is
good; abstain from every form of evil.*
1 Thessalonians 5:19-22

★ ★ ★

They're all found in the Old Testament, and they went by names like
Hosea, Joel, Amos, Obadiah, Jonah, Micah, Nahum, Habakkuk,
Zephaniah, Haggai, Zechariah, and Malachi, just to name a few. They were
often called Seers, Servants, Messengers, Men of God and Sons of
Prophets. Their purpose was to "edify" the people to whom they spoke.
Proofs of a true prophet were: (read Deuteronomy 18:15-22).

#1 Speak in the name of Yahweh
#2 Speak by revelation or inspiration
#3 Moral character of the prophet
#4 A true call of God
#5 A message authenticated by signs
#6 A message in agreement with previous revelation
#7 The fulfillment of predictions

What I don't want to get into during this devotional time is trying to
answer the question, "Is there modern day prophecy?" or "Are there modern day prophets?" What I do want to touch on is verifying the true from
the false. The list from Deuteronomy 18 makes clear what constitutes a
true prophet of God. But we must beware because a false prophet doesn't
prophesy in the name of a pagan god, but under the name of Yahweh (the
only God). Although this false prophet claims to speak in the name of
Yahweh, he/she will not hold up when compared to the above proofs of
a true prophet. The New Testament continually warns us of "wolves
dressed in sheep's clothes," and "good and bad trees." Be careful what you
take as fact and learn to discern truth from error. As James warns us in
chapter 1 verse 16, "Don't be easily deceived fellow believers!" Remember
that everyone on earth is fallen (Romans 3:23) and needs the power of
God and the accountability of the scripture. Make sure you test what people teach from the Bible. False teaching leads to false theology, which ultimately leads to a false religion. Take heed!

★ ★ ★

Further Study: How do you separate biblical truth from secular theology?

THE LION IN DANIEL'S DEN

Then the king was pleased and gave orders for Daniel to be taken up out of the den, and no injury whatever was found on Daniel because he had trusted in his God.
Daniel 6:23

★ ★ ★

My wife and I named our oldest son Daniel for a reason. I love the story of a man in the Bible named Daniel who stood strong in the midst of great adversity. To fully appreciate the story of how Daniel escaped unharmed from the lions' den, you must first know a few facts about a lion. Contrary to how Simba was portrayed in Disney's movie, *Lion King,* a lion in the wild is a predator and aggressor, the dominator of his land. Lions have a keen sense of hearing and eyesight and are quick as a snake and strong as Hercules. Lions will only attack their prey from behind, not straight on. That's why they feed at night and rest during the hot African days. Surprise is their greatest asset, and they use it regularly to maintain their "King of the Beasts" title.

Daniel was wise beyond his years and needed that wisdom as he interpreted the dreams of Nebuchadnezzar (how is that for a long name?), the bad king of a bad place called Babylon. This king wanted everyone to worship a gold image or statue, but Daniel wouldn't because he had a different belief.

The world in which you and I live is always asking us to bow down and worship images in the form of money, appearance, where we live, power, lack of integrity or dishonesty. We, like Daniel, will be tested to see whose god we will follow. The real question is, do we believe so much in Christ that we are willing to take on any lion in our lives to show His faithfulness? Do we trust in God so much that we are more willing to stand alone for the truth than with the crowds in a lie? You will have these "tests of trust" throughout your life where you will have an opportunity to prove once again, as Daniel did, "Our God is an awesome God and He reigns in heaven and on earth."

★ ★ ★

Further Study: What does the world offer you as "good" that ultimately robs you of what's "great" with God? What did Daniel do to survive in the lions' den? How can you trust God in the face of adversity? What does trusting God mean to you?

TIME

And he will speak out against the Most High and wear down the saints of the Highest One, and he will intend to make alterations in times and in law; and they will be given into his hand for a time, times, and half a time.
Daniel 7:25

★ ★ ★

God created time and humans invented the watch. For thousands of years, human beings have been anxious about the time they have on earth. We all have a desire to live long and prosperous lives, yet there are no guarantees on how long our time will last (James 4:14). I love this life as much as the next person, yet the older I get (which is happening way too fast) and the more I read the scriptures, I realize this life is not gonna be a walk in the lily field. A life lived being a follower of Jesus Christ is gonna get tougher and harder the longer you walk. I admire men and women of God who started their journey at a young age and got up and kept going when they stumbled along the way. We here in America don't feel or see the persecution that so many brothers and sisters across the ocean feel daily. Our lives in the "Good Old U.S. of A" are pretty insulated from such aggression, yet I believe the scriptures indicate that "time" will come before Christ does.

Now this is not a devotion about a pre, mid or post-tribulation that believers will encounter, but it is a reality check on what we can expect. Daniel's interpretation of a vision was alarming to him and should be a wake-up call to us. We will, if we are producing spiritual fruit (Galatians 5:22-23), be persecuted for our faith in one form or another. It may be mental persecution rather than physical persecution, but mental persecution is painful, too. Daniel warns us that we will hear those who speak out against God and will experience a wearing down effect. Our country will be run by leaders with a game plan that is opposite ours and the journey will be long and weary. Enjoy the journey and cling tightly to righteousness. Live life with the realization that we will have an afterlife of hope without pain and sorrow. Keep your eyes on the prize.

★ ★ ★

Further Study: How do you feel when a non-believer makes fun of you for your faith? How can you remain strong? What is the purpose of trials and tribulation? How do they affect you? How do they affect your family?

Shoulder to Shoulder

It is not good for man to be alone.
Genesis 2:18

★ ★ ★

For South African President Nelson Mandela and his prison mates, keeping dignity intact required shared vision, commitment to bear one another's burdens, and strength to stand in unity no matter what the opposition. In *Time* magazine (Nov. 28, 1994) Mandela wrote, "The authorities' greatest mistake was keeping us together, for together our determination was reinforced. It would be very hard, if not impossible, for one man alone to resist. I do not know if I could have done it had I been alone. Whatever we learned, we shared, and by sharing we multiplied whatever courage we had individually. The stronger ones raised up the weaker ones and both became strong in the process."

What a powerful story, don't you think? What a tremendous lesson (and one we can learn without taking up residence in the pen) about staying shoulder to shoulder with other Christians in the midst of adversity. If God wanted us to be loners and have no fellowship, I think He would have put us each on our own planet to sit and rotate on our axis all our lonely lives. A ton of strength lies in those "friends that stick closer than any brother." Don't be fearful that it may take time to develop a shoulder-to-shoulder relationship with someone. Don't put off until tomorrow what can help you today. Don't make yourself out to be some super hero with an emblem on your chest. Don't be a cowboy (or girl) riding into the sunset alone, acting tough. Don't you hate reading the word "don't" 10 times straight? Okay, then just do it!

★ ★ ★

Further Study: Write down a list of your top 10 best friends (I'll wait). Okay, now which of these folks do you stand shoulder-to-shoulder with? Why or why not? How can you develop this today?

RIGHT TOOL, WRONG WAY

Come let us worship and bow down; let us kneel before
the Lord our maker for He is our God.
Psalm 95:6-7

★ ★ ★

In an issue of *Meat & Poultry* magazine, editors quoted *Feathers*, the publication of the California Poultry Industry Federation, telling the following story. It seems the U.S. Federal Aviation Administration has a unique device for testing the strength of windshields on airplanes. The device is a gun that launches a dead chicken at a plane's windshield at approximately the speed the plane flies. The theory is that if the windshield doesn't crack from the carcass impact, it will survive a real air collision with a bird during flight.

It seems the British were very interested in this and wanted to test a windshield on a brand new, speedy locomotive they were developing. They borrowed FAA's chicken launcher, loaded the chicken and fired.

The ballistic chicken shattered the windshield, broke the engineer's chair and embedded itself in the back wall of the engine cab. The British were stunned and asked the FAA to recheck the test to see if everything was done correctly.

The FAA reviewed the test thoroughly and had one recommendation: use thawed chickens!

What a hilarious story (true) of having the right tool, but using it the wrong way and the results thereof. This devotion is going to address the subject of "worship" both personally and corporately. The first question I have for you is "Do you worship God?" And my second question is "What are the motives behind your worship?" Contemporary churches today are really turning up the music in terms of bands and modern day lyrics to songs during singing at church. The meaning of worship is to "find worth in" what you're worshiping. In the Old Testament, believers worshiped through blood sacrifices and offerings. Today we seem to be falling into more of a "feeling" rather than a "realization" of worship. I'm not saying feeling is wrong, yet I am saying we need to come into worship with a sense of reverence and honor of the Holy One rather than only a "buddy" or "pal" mentality. Use your time alone or with others in worship as a personal time to honor and glorify your Savior and Lord, not as a time of false feeling and public display. Make sure you're living out privately what you're worshiping publicly.

★ ★ ★

Further Study: What does worship mean to you?

GOD'S CHARACTER

In wrath remember mercy.
Habakkuk 3:2

✭ ✭ ✭

Do you come from the same type of family I came from, where your mother represented TLC (Tender Loving Care) and sugar and your dad represented the heat and vinegar? Now I say that in all due respect, yet to prove a valuable point. Most of our parents served in a specific role in our growing up years. That role influenced how we think of our parents today.

We also have a particular view of God that has been influenced by our upbringing and culture. The problem is that the view we have may not be the complete truth. We don't often hear in our contemporary, padded pew churches that the God (Yahweh) of scripture is a God of, yes, love and mercy, but also of judgment and consequences. Now the reason we don't hear that much today is that it doesn't enlarge church attendance or make a good fundraising ploy. The true character of Yahweh is all four of those characteristics. Those qualities didn't change from the God of the Old Testament to the Jesus of the New Testament. In Revelation 5:5, Jesus Himself is called the "Lion of Judah." Correct me if I'm wrong, but I don't think lions make cuddly pets. Instead, they are well respected for their power and position.

Here's my point . . . we have a hard time in our western culture seeing or knowing of anyone who could possibly be tender yet firm. Usually people are seen as loving and merciful or as judgmental and abrasive, but not both. God's character is one to love and fear because He will either bless you because you obeyed or judge you with consequences because you disobeyed. That is the God of the Bible. Obedience to His Spirit and Holy Word are key to our future and happiness on this earth. Understanding fully the true character of God helps us to love, worship, pray to and obey Him more.

✭ ✭ ✭

Further Study: Describe your mother, then your father. How does your view of your parents influence your view of your heavenly Father? How can God be so balanced? Why does the Old Testament use the phrase "fear the Lord?"

17

WHO AM I, LORD?

*Now as they observed the confidence of Peter and John and understood that
they were uneducated and untrained men, they were marveling,
and began to recognize them as having been with Jesus.*
Acts 4:13

★ ★ ★

Verbal slams on intelligence are as common as flies on a cow. Check
out a few bumper stickers I've seen recently that prove my point:

Your kid may be an honors student but you're still an idiot.
Forget about world peace . . . Visualize using your blinker.
We have enough youth, how about a fountain of smart?
He who laughs last thinks slowest.
Lottery: A tax on people who are bad at math.
All men are idiots and I married their king.
The more people I meet . . . the smarter my dog is.
I took an I.Q. test and the results were negative.

Fewer students graduate from college in only four years, and when
they do get out . . . they go right back in to get that masters. Our society
puts a very high value on education and intelligence, which is not necessarily wrong. However, it is wrong when society places a lower value on
morals and values. I have been taking classes at a local seminary and
noticed a spiritual arrogance among the students and teachers. I'm not
bashing the purpose of education or the value of learning, but I do know
that God and His divine intervention in a person's life through faithfulness
and obedience is really what needs to be looked up to and admired. In the
above scripture, here are Peter and John, two fishermen who didn't get an
MBA or a masters degree in theology or fishing, yet were chosen as two
of twelve to "be" with Christ. Why? Because they were willing and obedient to their call (Luke 5:11). God's eyes search near and far for those
under-qualified, under-gifted, under-achievers to live out His glory and
power through them. Are you someone who feels God is lucky to have
you on His team or are you the one questioning if God could ever use
someone like you? I'll let you do the math and figure out which one He'll
choose. Until next time . . . keep walking in His Spirit and spending daily
time in His Word.

★ ★ ★

Further Study: Why does our culture put such a huge emphasis on education and not Christ-like qualities?

GLEANING

He who is faithful in a very little is faithful also in much.
Luke 16:10

★ ★ ★

Webster defines gleaning as "gathering grain (leftovers or scraps) or other produce left behind by the reapers." I saw peasants gleaning in the fields in the third world country of Haiti. You don't have to go far in our country to find street people or beggars gleaning for a morsel of food or left-over soda in a thrown away fast food container.

The book of Ruth tells a great story. The scene begins with Ruth, the Moabitess, asking Naomi (her mother-in-law) for permission to be "lowly" and go to the fields to glean a meal. To make this story short and get to the application, Ruth, by her willingness to be lowly and work hard, meets a wealthy man named Boaz, who ends up marrying Ruth. Together they have a son and live happily ever after.

Now my point here is not to show you an early "Leave it to Beaver" family, but to outline how Ruth got from point "A" of gleaning to point "B" of happiness and fulfillment. Let's take a quick look at how this progression was achieved by Ruth:

verse 2:1 Ruth had a proper perspective of God and His faithfulness to us.
verse 2:2 Ruth was faithful in the small areas and respectful to others.
verse 2:3 Ruth was obedient and worked hard at what she could do.
verse 2:4 Ruth was faithful (loyal) for as long as God wanted her to glean.
verse 2:7 Ruth's faithfulness and hard work opened doors.

You see, God is more willing to lead you and me as we follow Him. God's work can be slow for a long time, then suddenly it can move quickly. God doesn't elevate foolish people to high positions. He won't guide you until He breaks you. The process can be ugly, but the results are beautiful. If you're lowly now and gleaning for all you can . . . press on, God is close by.

★ ★ ★

Further Study: Have you ever had to be lowly for a long period of time? How did you respond? Why does God really need to "bruise you before He can use you?"

UNCHANGING WORD IN A CHANGING WORLD

Who will dwell on Thy holy hill? He who walks with integrity and works righteousness and speaks truth in his heart.
Psalm 15:1-2

★ ★ ★

I absolutely love the way biblical accounts play out to a plot, as well as the lessons you and I learn from them and can apply today. Take a minute and read the story found in 1 Kings 22:1-38 and I'll be here when you come   back . . . go on. Welcome back. Now was that awesome or what? Did Micaiah the prophet go into this scene lookin' foolish and come out smelling like a rose or what? Today, politicians say whatever they need to get the votes; media plays to the audience and our culture applauds. Where are those few who are willing to "stand alone" in the midst of the firing squad? There is a country song that says, "You've got to stand for something or you'll fall for anything." Micaiah had Ahab, the king of Israel, and Jehoshaphat, the King of Judah, along with 400 prophet puppets breathing down his neck to prophesy falsely and fold under the pressure. Did he, though? No! This man of God was willing to take verbal, physical and mental abuse for the cause of Yahweh (God). He knew his role and continued to play the lead until his prophecy came true in verses 37-38. Here are a few lessons I personally learned from this nugget of scripture. Feel free to add to them:

#1 It is better to be divided by the truth than be united in compromise.
#2 It is better to speak biblical truth that heals than lies that kill.
#3 It is better to be hated for standing for truth than for telling a lie.
#4 It is better to be lonely in the truth than with the multitudes in a lie.
#5 It is better to ultimately succeed with truth than succeed in a lie.

Don't forget that Noah went into the ark a minority with only his family, but 40 days later . . . he came out a majority. You and I need to be the ones that stand firm (and sometimes alone) for what's right. This world needs to see disciples of Christ standing for Christ-like principles in a world that approves of abortions, ungodly movies and music, broken commitments and promises. The scriptures are full of men and women who held tight to truth in the midst of turbulent tests and trials, and that legacy can continue if you choose to be a modern day Micaiah.

★ ★ ★

Further Study: What's the scariest part about standing alone?

FIRE IT UP!

*Finally Christian, we request you in the Lord that as you received from us
instructions as to how to walk and please God that you may excel still more.*
1 Thessalonians 4:1

★ ★ ★

Catch the jingle of this tune: "Enthusiasm, it's the bread of life, like
protoplasm, one, two, three, four, five, it's great to be alive because I've
got . . . enthusiasm." (catchy, ain't it). Dale Carnegie said, "A person can
accomplish almost anything for which he has unlimited enthusiasm."
Thomas Edison was quoted, "If all we leave to our kids is enthusiasm,
we've left them an estate of incalculable value." It won't be education, con-
nections or the way you dress that get you there . . . it will be those who
are excited about something who will go farthest in life. When you
become an excited person, you will have an exciting life. When you actually get excited about your career, marriage and/or friendships, you will
have an exciting career, marriage and/or friendships. To change your attitude, which is the ignition of enthusiasm, you start with a change in behavior. Begin to act the part of the person you'd rather be or become and grad-
ually the old person with no spark will fade out of the picture.

A couple of key points to remember as you become more excited about
life!
    #1 Change your bad attitude
    #2 Fake joy is better than genuine depression
    #3 Claim victory and take ownership
    #4 Don't let your feelings become facts
    #5 Winners never quit and quitters never win

Four beliefs worth believing as you go:
    #1 Belief in God gives you a sense of purpose
    #2 Belief in yourself gives you confidence
    #3 Belief in others gives you relationships
    #4 Belief in what you do gives you enthusiasm

Life really is, when you think about it, so simple. Life is energy. It is
our use of that energy that influences the circumstances and situations of
our lives. If you want to change the direction of your life, all you need to
do is change your energy level. So . . . "get fired up!"

★ ★ ★

Further Study: What gets you excited about life?

21

GOD-GIVEN GIFTS

A man's gift makes room for him and brings him before great men.
Proverbs 18:16

★ ★ ★

A raccoon is equipped with special reflective cells which are located at the rear of his eyes. This apparatus allows the coon to see in partial darkness. Light enters the eyes of the animal and is absorbed. The light that is not absorbed is reflected by these "mirror cells" and it again passes through the retina, giving this light another chance to be absorbed. Through this mirroring device, "tapetum lucidum," the raccoon is able to use what limited light the night has to hunt and move around.

I lived in southwest Missouri for 13 years where a popular pastime is coon huntin' in the wee hours of the morning. The coon dogs are let go by their owner (the hunter) to track and tree the raccoon (the hunted). The whole time you hear these huntin' dogs yelping in the hills and woods, telling their master the location of the coon through the pitch of their howls (bark). Once the coon is treed, the hunter can quickly locate the animal up in the giant oaks by shining a flashlight up into the tree and picking up the reflective glow off the eyes of the coon.

One of the best tips of marital wisdom I ever got was at a FamilyLife Conference. It was this, "What lures you (attracts) to your spouse during courtship can repel (separate) you during marriage." So the reflective eyes of the raccoon, an obvious gift of nature, end up being the very thing that leads the raccoon to its death. How can a strength become a weakness? How can a gift become a gag? I'll tell ya' what this old cowboy thinks . . . worldliness and darkness take control instead of the Spirit of righteousness and light. A good tool for you becomes a weapon for the enemy; ironic, ain't it? Beware, my friend, and take warning . . . Satan is out to kill and destroy you in whatever deceptive way possible.

★ ★ ★

Further Study: What do you feel are your greatest gifts personally? Have you ever used them for dishonest gain? How can you use your God-given gifts and talents only for the Kingdom?

PREPARE THE WAY

*"What do I have to do with you, Jesus, Son of the Most High God? Do not tor-
ment me!" And the demons entreated Him saying, "Send us into the swine."*
Mark 5:7, 12

✳ ✳ ✳

It was probably early the next morning that they came to see; by this
time, the Gadarene had dressed and gotten cleaned up and was sitting
with Jesus and the disciples (Mark 5:15). The men were fearful and asked
Jesus to leave, maybe because of a lost herd of pigs, maybe because of
someone possessing supreme power in their midst. In this Greek city of
Decapolis they were ignorant of spiritual truth and infested with pagan
superstition. There is a contrast here between the attitude of the men and
the attitude of the one who was rid of his demons. They begged Jesus to
leave, while the healed man begged to stay with Jesus and was refused. He
probably feared that if Jesus left him the demons would enter his body
again, or he felt acceptance and safety with his newfound master.
Understand this, he had been an outcast from his friends for such a long
time, and it was tough for him to be denied fellowship with the One who
made him whole and happy again. The reason Jesus told him "no," but to
go home and tell his friends of what great thing had happened to him
(Mark 5:19), was that these folks needed evidence that the Lord would not
only do miracles, but could permanently transform a life.

It seems like a great story with a rotten punch line. Why so mean,
Jesus? Let the guy stay with ya', Jesus. He had been healed, yet Jesus did
with him what He did with the demons . . . cast em' out. The reality of this
story is that there was much more to be done than casting out demons
into some smelly swine herd. The real story was just about to begin, as this
Gadarene man was commanded to spread the good news in a Greek area
where Jesus was not very welcome. When the Lord returned to that area
later, He was warmly received because of the footwork this man had done.
Why? The Gadarene had prepared the way for Him and now Jesus was
able to go to work in their midst (Mark 7:31-37). Maybe it's a club, team,
business, social group or peer clique that God is asking you to go into and
proclaim truth. Then His Spirit can go to town transforming lives. Are you
willing to take that step of faith to see lives saved and changed, or are you
scared of losing face in front of your peers and friends? Go ahead . . . make
that move!

✳ ✳ ✳

Further Study: Are you, like the Gadarene, willing to go into uncomfortable
areas to proclaim good news?

PASSED DOWN

This I command you, that you love one another just as I (Jesus) have loved you.
John 15:12

★ ★ ★

It has the same potential for destruction as any of the terrorist bombings in Beirut, Manhattan or Oklahoma City. It's a bomb all right, hidden in the heart of a majority of the world's population. If not defused, it could send us all flying from an explosion of domestic violence and inherited anger. This bomb is called racism. The blood-poisoning of ignorance, misinformation, hate and anger has been passed down from generation to generation. White, black, yellow or brown–we must forget the past and stop using that as fuel for our present beliefs. God put us all on one planet for a reason. Let me inject this vaccine into your thinking. You won't overcome the hate and anger stemming from racism without a strong dose of Jesus in your heart. I direct an inner-city camp called "The Sky's the Limit" in the five points region ("the Hood") of Denver. It has been a huge education for me to get involved with "the Hood" and the youth who live there. Love is the bridge that allows all colors to come together before anger, hate and revenge take the spot. No matter your background, you have the capability to stop the thinking passed down from generations past. Open your heart to Christ's renewing love and educate yourself. Cross-cultural friendships can be some of the most rewarding you'll ever make. Serving a minority, feeding the poor and hungry, volunteering your time and labor to a cause is what Christianity is made of. Be a part of the solution, not the problem, and be a catalyst (leader) in putting an end to racism.

★ ★ ★

Further Study: Do you think that racism is a problem? Why? Why not? Do you see yourself as a racist? Do you have friends of another color? What can you do to be a part of the solution, not the problem, of racism?

KEEP ON KEEPING ON

Beloved, do not be surprised at the fiery ordeal among you, which comes upon you for your testing, as though some strange thing were happening to you.
1 Peter 4:12

★ ★ ★

I've been on a horse at the middle fork of the Salmon River, northwest of Challis, Idaho, in the Salmon National Forest. The Salmon River empties into the Snake River, which then flows into the Columbia River that empties into the Pacific Ocean just north of Portland, Oregon. The king salmon (fish) begins its journey from the ocean and salt water to the place it hatched years before in freshwater rivers. Facing overwhelming odds, this fish doggedly fights its way upstream, returning to its original spawning grounds. The salmon will travel some 25 miles each day, fighting a rough current and predators, while relying on rays of the moon and sun to navigate. This trip can take up to six months and many missed meals. When the salmon arrives, the males battle against each other for territorial rights. Each February, pale orange eggs hatch after lying on the bottom of the riverbed during the winter. Lying along the gravel of the river bottom, eggs are vulnerable to other fish and birds. Only about 10 percent end up hatching and beginning their journey back to the ocean, repeating this incredible cycle.

This natural struggle and determination is what make king salmon (all 50 to 100 pounds) one of the most highly prized game and commercial fish in North America. The struggle and barriers along this migratory journey serve as a way to strengthen the fish for tougher battles and obstacles ahead. You and I tend to view tough, turbulent times as unfortunate or inconvenient, yet God's plan is to test us so we and He can see what we need to work on and what areas need improvement. Christ never said that following Him was gonna be a walk in the park. Just as taking a test in school helps you and the teacher find out how many of the lessons are learned, so it is in God's classroom, which can't be taken via correspondence or by using Cliff Notes. The upstream waters in our life will be turbulent with trials, but the destination is heavenly.

★ ★ ★

Further Study: Why are endurance and perseverance as important for believers as they are to the migration of the king salmon?

25

DUELING

Be angry yet don't sin; Don't let the sun go down on your
anger, and don't give the devil an opportunity.
Ephesians 4:26-27

★ ★ ★

It took place on a hill overlooking the Hudson River between two statesmen (politicians) on July 11, 1804. Both represented our political system, one an honored Democrat, the other a noble Republican. They differed in their personal ways of handling conflict, yet this meeting on July 11th proved fatal. Their names: Aaron Burr and Alexander Hamilton. The straw that broke the camel's back was a letter that Hamilton published in a newspaper in New Jersey to air out his distrust and dissatisfaction of the job Burr had been doing on Capitol Hill. Burr read the article and became furious, challenging Hamilton to a pistol duel. Hamilton was a church-going, Bible-believing Christian whose character wouldn't allow him to handle disagreements in this manner, especially a shoot out. Just three years earlier, Philip, Alexander's son, was killed in a duel because of his beliefs. At the duel in 1804, Alexander was killed by Burr because Alexander shot his pistol in the air, not at Burr.

Not much has changed in almost 200 years. Many still resolve differences with violence. Television programs, movies, gangster rap and militia magazines all try to sway us towards violence. Our inner cities are war zones of fist fights and drive-by shootings. Our "right to bear arms" has turned into a "license to kill." Jesus had, and still has, another means for His followers to resolve disagreements. How? Read Ephesians 6:13-17. Notice that of all the armor only one piece is offensive; the others are defensive (or to protect us). God's Word is our weapon, not a rifle, pistol, bomb, fist, knife, or sharp tongue. Jesus exemplified this tactic when He Himself was in arms against the devil's temptations. God's Word and His Spirit are all we have, but they are also all we need. A word of caution about our tongues . . . it's the only instrument that the more you use it, the sharper it becomes!

★ ★ ★

Further Study: How do you and your family resolve conflict? Is your first instinct to lash out with your tongue? How do you handle your anger? Snap? Hit? Backbite? Stuff it? Run? How can you and your family handle arguments better? Will you?

26

SEARCH FOR SIGNIFICANCE

You made all the delicate, inner parts of my body
and knit them together in my mother's womb.
Psalm 139:13

☆ ☆ ☆

Why do we search for our personal significance through places, positions and people? We base our value and our worth on everything but truth. I sure don't want to sound preachy, but we need to get back to the basics. We need to let truth grab our hearts and change how we act and think! If we can change the way we think, we will act differently.

Let's go over some basics. Did God need humans? Absolutely not! But He obviously thought there was some worth in our existence because He chose to use us. Did God have the ultimate veto power in deciding if you should have been born, no matter what the circumstance? You had better say, "Absolutely!" Okay, through the process of elimination, there is a very good reason for you being born. You are significant, and there is a reason for you being on this earth and/or in your particular family.

If you said "yes" to God needing humans or "no" to God being able to veto our births, then you are saying something very serious about God–that He is a liar! The Book of John tells us that He is Truth. God is completely incapable of lying. He has no ability in any way to lie! And if you don't believe the Word of God, then pray! God says that if we seek the truth, we will find it.

God has created us with the ability to get to know Him intimately, but we need to read His love letter. Psalm 139 reminds us that He knows everything about us . . . and He still loves us (you). That's a forgiving God. The Living Bible says, "How precious it is, Lord, to realize that you're thinking about me constantly. I can't even count how many times a day your thoughts turn towards me." That is awesome. Search Him, and let Him remind you how very precious you are to Him.

☆ ☆ ☆

Further Study: What does the world say about you and your worth? How does this contrast with what God says? Which will you choose and why?

27

GOD WORKS DESPITE US

If I have all faith, so as to remove mountains, but do not have love, I'm nothing.
1 Corinthians 13:2

★ ★ ★

Does God place an unbelievable amount of significance on love or what? Wow, take a look at 1 Corinthians chapter 13. These aren't things like taking the trash out for your mom, or helping grandma across the street. These acts are monumental; for example, verse 1, "speaks with the tongues of men and angels;" verse 2, "prophecy;" verse 3, "know all mysteries and all knowledge, faith to remove mountains;" verse 4, "give everything to the poor, sacrifice my body." Can you believe what God is saying?! He is making a very strong point. He wants us to exemplify that same kind of love!

What is amazing about these verses is they prove to us that God is going to work despite what we do or don't do. He is a sovereign God; what He wants done, He will get done with or without us! And isn't it awesome that He does work despite us. If God really needed us, we would mess up all kinds of projects (not to mention what it says about God if He needs us. If God really needs us, then He is not all powerful, all knowing, sovereign and many other things that God says He is!)

Okay, so let's get practical. God is probably not going to ask us to move a mountain, or speak with the tongues of angels (although nothing is impossible with God). What does God ask of us? He asks us to be patient, kind, not jealous, not arrogant. He asks us not to be unbecoming, not to seek our own desires, not to take account of a wrong, etc. Truth be known, a lot of times these things are extremely difficult. We might rather have God ask us to move a mountain than not seek our own desires or not remain angry at something someone did to us.

Paul's point is clear in 1 Corinthians 13: show your love not in huge and great acts, but in everyday acts with kindness and patience to those with whom you are surrounded. "The greatest of these is love."

★ ★ ★

Further Study: What kinds of things have you done out of selfishness and not love? Are you taking account of any wrongs suffered that you need to forgive? Why is it harder to show 1 Corinthians 13 love to our families than to anyone else?

A FINAL FAREWELL

I know you will bring me down to death a place appointed to all the living.
JOB 30:23

✫ ✫ ✫

In the game of life we must all make many important choices. There is one door that we all will go through without a choice . . . death. I think the "reality check" we all feel when we go to a funeral is that at some unannounced moment in our lives, we too, will pass through that door. In a world of advancing technology, medicine and cultural predictability, we haven't quite figured out God's timing. Whether we're young and full of energy like Princess Diana, who died unexpectedly at age 36, or like Mother Teresa, who had lived a fulfilling life to age 87, death is unpredictable. Death seems to surround itself with friends like grief, mourning, tears, questions, nervousness, anxiety, surprise and hopelessness, yet it shouldn't if eternal life is the big picture. Death of a pagan and death of a believer in Jesus Christ are on separate ends of the emotional scale. They both include loss and sorrow, yet only one has inner peace and eternal hope.

I heard a quote one time that said, "hell, some people believe in it, some people don't; someday they will." You don't hear much these days being taught on the subject of heaven and hell. Upon entering the tunnel of mortal death, we all will come out in either of those two final resting places. One will be a destination of eternal pain, torment and unrest called hell. The second being a divine paradise, lacking pain and sorrow, yet consisting of peaceful joy, happiness and eternity with the God of the Universe called heaven. Gang, no one has the corner on the market of time, nor a guarantee of length of life. Once you pass through those unappeasable doors, you live with the decisions of belief you came in with. There will be no turning back; the hands of time and life will continue on. Cultivate daily your faith in Christ, your friendships in the faith and your family. Leave a legacy of heavenly love that will endure long after you leave. All our clocks are ticking, and when God your Father decides your clock should stop, either slowly or suddenly, and you have your final farewell . . . will you be ready? Will your death signify the beginning of a better life ahead? Invest in the present, and don't bank on your future. It won't be what you did outwardly, but who you are inwardly that will count at your final farewell.

✫ ✫ ✫

Further Study: How does talking about death make you feel? If you were to die suddenly today like Princess Diana, where would you go . . . heaven or hell? Why? How do you know you will go to heaven? Read John 4:14.

YOKE FELLOW

Jesus said to the twelve, "You don't want to go away also, do you?"
John 6:67

★ ★ ★

What a question to ask your teammates. Jesus has such a way of simplifying the process and getting to the point. The disciples knew who Jesus was, yet He wanted to know . . . would they leave? Peter saw Christ as someone to give eternal salvation to him and the world, yet Jesus wants us to see Him as more than a savior. He wants to be yoke fellows with us. Ironically, after Jesus asked this many of His disciples went back and walked no more with Him.

So many folks today focus so much of their attention on doing "things" and "services" for the cause of Christ, yet they don't walk with Him. God desires that we be one with Christ, not only in deed, but in passion and dependence. Don't try to live life with God on any other terms than His terms.

So what? How do we truly learn to walk with Jesus on a daily basis? What do we need to give up to do so? Our Lord wants us to let go before He can lay hold. He doesn't want our goodness, honesty or good deeds, but our sin. That's right, the sins we all possess so He can exchange them for real righteousness. Are you willing to relinquish all pretense of being anything or of deserving God's love? God's Spirit will guide us to which sin we need to give up. It may come in the form of possessions, power or position. There is always a painful disillusionment we go through before we do the relinquishing. When we see ourselves as the Lord sees us, it's not the abominable sins of the flesh that shock us, but the awful nature of pride in our own hearts against Christ. That's when conviction takes place. Be a follower of Jesus who will stick with Him through the good and bad times. Do you want to be a true "yoke fellow" and join up with Jesus on your journey through life? It will cost you today, but pay big dividends in the future. It may seem like it's costly today, but believe me, the dividends in the future are worth it.

★ ★ ★

Further Study: Why is it so hard to walk daily with Christ? How does sin hinder our walk like a nail in the bottom of our hiking boot on a campout? Today, what would be the hardest thing for you to relinquish to God in order to walk closer with Him?

THE LONG HAUL

*He was faithful to Him who appointed Him, as Moses also was in his own
house.*
Hebrews 3:2

★ ★ ★

Moses was born in a country that had banned his own birth. His
mother, to protect him, floated him down the Nile River. Moses was found
by Pharaoh's daughter, and she adopted him as her own. Ironically,
Pharaoh's daughter hired Moses' birth mother to nurse him, not knowing
Moses was her son. Moses was raised like a king in soft beds, eating royal
food, yet in a palace void of spiritual influence. In spite of this environment,
he learned skills of military science, useful in organizing a group of slaves
into an army. Years in the desert of Midian taught Moses to serve sheep,
his family and father-in-law, and deepened his communion with God. He
learned the skills of nomadic survival which helped him as he led three
million slaves in the Sinai Peninsula for 40 years. Now he was ready for the
task God had called him to after 80 years of training. In Exodus 14:16 we
read how God used Moses to divide the Red Sea and lead the Israelites to
safety while watching the Egyptian army all drown. Moses was to lead
these people to the Land of Milk and Honey (Promised Land), yet he was
forbidden by the Lord to enter the land and see his goal achieved. He died
in the land of Moab, disappointed. He pleaded three times for this not to
happen, yet was told by God not to mention his request anymore
(Deuteronomy 3:26). More than a thousand years later, however, his
request was granted on the Mount of Transfiguration when two men
talked with Jesus whose glory had been unveiled. One was Elijah, the other
Moses (Luke 9:31). Moses had been divinely escorted into the Promised
Land at last.

You see, Moses was one of the first to know about the Lord's plan of
redemption through the death, burial and resurrection of Jesus. Moses had
led the hard-to-manage, whiny-baby Israelites out of Egypt's slavery and
now knew how Jesus was gonna lead others out of the bondage of sin into
His Promised Land called heaven. God's timing is perfect yet unpredictable. We want to get instant gratification for a life lived in faithfulness
to God! We have a tendency to believe that if we don't get rewarded today
for our efforts, God will forget or overlook us. I tell you the truth, if you
live a life of sincere faith and trust in Christ, your rewards will come in
time, just maybe not on your time-table. Rewards will come; press on.

★ ★ ★

Further Study: Why did Moses have to go through so much training?

JUST FORGET IT!

Forgetting what lies behind and reaching forward to what lies ahead.
Philippians 3:13

★ ★ ★

It wouldn't be a true family devotional book unless I included a devotion about the family I grew up with in Dallas, Texas. You could describe my family as extremely athletic and pedigree potent. My mother (half Native American) was an all-state basketball player in high school. My father grew up in Oklahoma (he's an Okie) in a very poor family. His room was a screened-in porch (got cold in the winter, I bet) and he picked cotton and worked at his dad's feed store to help make ends meet. The only way he would get to go to college was if he earned a football scholarship out of Norman High School. My father did just that; he was a high school football star and signed with the University of Oklahoma to play for legendary coach Bud Wilkinson in 1954. My dad was a running back his first two years, then moved to starting quarterback his junior and senior years. Now get this, from the time my dad started his career at Oklahoma to the time he ended his career there, his record was 47 wins in a row and 1 loss. That final loss came in the last game of his college career against Notre Dame in the Orange Bowl in 1958 . . . 7–0. All along the way he won tons of honors, not to mention two national championships. This record of 47–1 still stands today as the longest winning streak in college football history. My dad went on to a professional football career in Canada, Dallas and Kansas City with the NFL.

Today, in my father's hay barn in Weatherford, Texas, you'll find boxes of dusty trophies, medals, ribbons and certificates; piles of sports pages honoring him; two solid bronze national championship trophies and his dinged up Oklahoma helmet, all with bird dung on them. Why? My dad is extremely humble and takes to heart not living in his past. My dad has every earned right to display his honors and hang out at the athletic departments in Norman and check out all those pictures of him and his team. Their record will never be beat. Carl Ray Dodd is a legend in football history, yet he doesn't know it. I'm not saying it's wrong to display your accomplishments or feel proud of your honors, but it's nice to know that there are some folks (few) out there not signing their own autographs, living in their past or reminding you just how great they are or were. I'm proud that one of those few is my dad.

★ ★ ★

Further Study: Why does scripture tell us to forget the past? Do you? Why is humility so meaningful to God?

THE PROMISE

*I set my bow in the cloud, and it shall be a sign
of a covenant between me and the earth.*
Genesis 9:13

★ ★ ★

I don't know if we can ever really understand what Noah must have gone through with the flood, followed by God giving him the promise "that all flesh shall never again be cut off by the water of the flood, neither shall there again be a flood to destroy the earth" (verse 11). That promise was not only for Noah and his family, but for us as well.

Do we really comprehend how much God loves us that He might give us promises? One of Webster's definitions of promise is: "a legally binding declaration that gives the person to whom it is made a right to expect or to claim the performance or forbearance of a specified act!" Hence, the person on the receiving end will benefit from the person making the promise. However, the person giving the promise has a huge responsibility to uphold his legally binding declaration. If God is who He says He is, He cannot come back on His word; that's not a part of His character.

Meditate on these promises and take God at His word . . .

- Do not tremble or be dismayed for the Lord your God is with you wherever you go. (Joshua 1:9)
- The Lord will accomplish what concerns me. (Psalm 138:8)
- And in Thy book they were all written, the days that were ordained for me, even before there was one of them. (Psalm 139:16)
- Train up a child in the way he should go, even when he is old he will not depart from it. (Proverbs 22:6)
- My sheep hear my voice and I know them . . . no one will snatch them out of my hand. (John 10:27-28)
- Walk by the Spirit and you will not carry out the desire of the flesh. (Galatians 5:16)
- Consider it joy when you encounter trials, knowing that the testing of your faith produces endurance and its perfect result . . . perfect and complete lacking in nothing. (James 1:2-4)

There are thousands more promises . . . so get in the Word and search for His promises. They will lift your spirit . . .. I promise!

★ ★ ★

Further Study: Which promises do you dwell on the most?

FALSE PRETENSE

And God saw all that He had made, and behold, it was very good.
Genesis 1:31

★ ★ ★

I know you don't care about this ancient history, but I need you to read on in order to make a spiritual point. When I was playing basketball at the University of Oklahoma, I was almost treated as a god in that state. I know that the only claim to fame for the state of Oklahoma was generated out of the musical starring Gordon McCrae and Shirley Jones, so it doesn't take much in the state to get attention. My point is this . . . it was fun to be so popular and high profile at the age of 20, but those feelings are fleeting and life goes on. The problem comes when most of my teammates who are now around 40 moved back to Norman, Oklahoma, to try and dip back into the past. It's tough to move away from those "Utopia times" when life seems to be a continual mountain top experience. The apostle Paul said, "Forget what lies behind and press on into the present and future" (Philippians 3:13). There is something in all of us, a longing, that we try to fill with a false pretense that there really is a "Garden of Eden" in a remote location somewhere in the world.

The beef I have about old teammates not moving on coincides with Christians in our culture pretending that a utopia exists somewhere in this world when it doesn't. There is not today, nor will there ever be, a perfect garden with no weeds this side of heaven. heaven is our hope and the gate we arrive at when we leave this world. Why in the world is everyone trying to get back into Genesis chapters 1 and 2 before sin enters the scene and destroys the plot of humanity? We desire a garden with no weeds. However, our job today is to face up to the fact that there are and always will be weeds (sin); we need to stop wishing and start pulling weeds in our world. Christians need to come back to the reality of a fallen world and a future place of hope, and not confuse the location of each. The reality of it all is that as bad as the world is, heaven looks better and better.

★ ★ ★

Further Study: Read Genesis 3:1-19 and discuss its ramifications. Why will this world today not ever be heaven? What should your job be while on earth? (Read Genesis 3:23.) What are the weeds in your own garden?

FAMILY FEUD

By wisdom a house is built, and by understanding it is established.
Proverbs 24:3

★ ★ ★

The sun was warm as it shone on the red, orange and brown leaves of the trees along the Tug River separating Kentucky and West Virginia that Indian summer day in the 1800s. It was a day that started like many other days when two families, one from Kentucky and the other from West Virginia, got together to share friendship, food and drink. However, the jubilance of the day turned into anger and mistrust when they started eating and a member of the host family informed their guests (maybe after a bit of moonshine) that the roast pig set before them had been rustled (stolen). That was the day the Hatfield clan, headed by "Devil Anse" Hatfield, informed the McCoy clan, headed by Ole Ran'l McCoy, that they were eatin' one of their own prized pigs. The feud intensified when several of the Hatfields, who had been drinking, disrupted an election party. Ellison Hatfield was stabbed and two McCoy youngsters were killed in retaliation. What followed was one of the longest, bloodiest feuds on record that our country has ever remembered . . . even today.

The old Hatfield vs. McCoy feud has been a legend that has lived on forever. It's like the family that never lets it die. Living in a society where the "fast lane" seems to be getting "stressed" up with no place to go, it's no wonder we live in conflict. Marriages and families are falling apart because the participants don't want to work through disagreements or misunderstandings. Pseudo listening and misunderstandings can develop when two people are at opposite ends of the continuum. We have got to realize we are all fearfully and wonderfully made (Psalm 139) and allow freedom for differences in styles and expressiveness. Our personal programming, self-images, false concepts and distrust hinder our relationships. We need to learn to appreciate differences; listen better; respect others' thoughts, feelings and needs; and realize communication is a life-long process. There are no quick fixes or simplified formulas, just a willing heart and an understanding of God's grace. Don't let ant hills of conflict become mountains of separation. Be bound and determined to do whatever it takes to end the feud.

★ ★ ★

Further Study: Why does God desire we live in harmony? What is the source of most of your family's feuds? How does your family peacefully resolve a feud? Take a look at the following scriptures and discuss each one of them: Ecclesiastes 3:1, 7 and James 1:19.

PAGAN ADORATION

Therefore, my beloved, flee from idolatry.
1 Corinthians 10:14

★ ★ ★

The best definition I have heard to describe an idol would be "anything that demands and gets their adoration." In lay terms . . . anything you or I adore above God is an idol. This form of false idol worship didn't just jump into our culture recently like a new fad. The Old Testament is full of kings like Nebuchadnezzar, the commander and chief of the Babylonian army, who was used as an instrument of judgment by God for His chosen disobedient people (Israelites). King "Neb" wanted his people to bow down to a god of gold. In our society today we don't have to look hard, or far, to see idolatry. In our western civilization we worship things like cars, houses, power, people (movie stars and athletes) and places. We see it in our world as countries still worship military power; pagan gods, such as those in the Hindu religion; dead gods, like Buddha; or stars in the sky.

We have become obsessed with all other gods rather than the true God. Why? Because the adoration of a false, pagan god requires no change or commitment. Yahweh doesn't choose to deal with idolatry lightly or overlook this sin. If we study the Old Testament, we'll see God judged harshly this type of worship with death, natural disasters and plagues. The idols may have changed, but the method behind the means hasn't. God is and will continue to judge our nation for its idolatry, and you and me, too, in order to bring us to a point of repentance (back home to Him). Take a look at your personal life and see what people, places or things have moved Jesus down on the priority pole (Matthew 6:24). Do you struggle with adoring and worshiping your job, money, appearance, body, children, spouse, friends, house, car, intellectual capabilities, an animal, sports, nature and celebrities more than your Savior? If so, you need to prioritize your adoration. Our God is a jealous God and requires all time, talents and treasures (Joshua 24:19). He will use whatever means He must to get your attention and adoration back.

★ ★ ★

Further Study: In view of historical biblical accounts of idolatry, why does scripture say, "a dog will return to his vomit?" Read Galatians 5:20-21 and see the importance of staying away from idol worship. What do you personally struggle with as an idol? Are you willing to change? When?

LET GO AND LET GOD

She came to Him and began to bow down before Him, saying, "Lord help me!"
Matthew 15:25

✬ ✬ ✬

You've heard the phrase "let go and let God" for years. I never really understood that principle until the summer of 1970 on a small island in the middle of Lake Texoma where some friends and I would go hang out during the summer. I was only 12 at the time and about as smart as a box of rocks. My three friends, Bobby, Jeff, Billy and I were doing our best to recreate an old war movie we saw the night before. I remember a large mound of sand that must have piled up from high water which we decided would be great to tunnel through to make a series of connecting fox holes. My buddies were gathering some tree limbs while I, the macho nacho, was digging this termite tunnel. As you have probably figured out by now, sand is the worst to try to dig in, because it has no strength to hold up walls. The tunnel collapsed on me, so all that was left showing was my Chuck Taylor basketball shoes. Immediately my vision became blackness and the oxygen became non-existent. I'm sorry to say I lost it and panicked. I began to kick, scream, twist and turn like a wind-up toy gone mad. My friends returned to find me trapped and tried to grab my feet and pull me out backwards. There was only one small problem . . . they couldn't catch my feet, because I was kicking like an Olympic swimmer. Finally, after I had used all the air left in that pocket, I passed out, at which time my friends could free me from the hole.

How many times in our lives do we kick, twist, rant and rave in a situation before we finally let go and let God? God seems to always be there at the right time, but we seem to think we wear an "S" on our chest and can "get out of this ourselves." Why is it that there are always two ways to do things, our way and the right way? Allow God to take control of your life in chaos without kicking Him away. All He wants to do is help us out of our holes, and all we need to do is relax and let Him. Take it from an ex-foxhole digger . . . it sure is good to see the light at the end of the tunnel.

✬ ✬ ✬

Further Study: What holes have you dug yourself into lately? Are you kicking God or allowing Him to free you? Why or why not?

VERBAL ROAD SIGNS

Without consultation, plans are frustrated, but with many counselors, they succeed. Proverbs 15:22

★ ★ ★

If I had one dollar for every piece of false counsel I've received in my lifetime, I'd single-handedly make Fort Knox go belly-up. Seeking guidance, direction, opinions or advice on matters of importance in one's life can be a dangerous adventure. As you travel along life's journey of rock slides, sharp turns, steep grades, and uneven ground, you will value verbal road signs. Whether it's advice on a career change, marriage partner, financial investment, or simply a recommendation for a movie, you'll need direction. But be careful; when the wrong folks give counsel, it can cause real problems. Here is a quick lesson from people who are wise enough to give counsel–don't give it until asked (and then they'll probably get back to you after some thought and prayer). Wise counsel is not the answer to every problem, but good, thought-provoking questions cause you to re-evaluate a situation and think through the process.

This information is probably not news to you. I do think that we all should be very selective of those we choose to guide and direct our decisions. Set up a "personal advisory board" made up of three people. The following is a check-list of qualifications for your board members:

Must be over 40 years old.
Must be a Christian-Servant.
Must seek God daily through scripture study and prayer.
Must have at least one male and two females or two males and one female on the board.
Must have known you for at least five years.
Must use scripture-based precepts as basis for counsel.

Use this group (board) as a sounding board for all your major decisions. Pray about who should be on your board, then call and ask them to participate. Good luck!

★ ★ ★

Further Study: Ready to assemble a board? Who qualifies that you know? How can you go about asking them? What's the hold-up?

INTO-ME-SEE (INTIMACY)

Jonathan was knit to the soul of David, and
Jonathan loved him (David) *as himself.*
1 Samuel 18:1

★ ★ ★

It makes our lives happier, improves our daily productivity, boosts our confidence level and self-worth, and most importantly, strengthens our walk with God. This endangered species in the wilderness of words is intimacy, or into-me-see. Intimacy is the ability to experience an open, supportive, compassionate relationship with another person without fear of condemnation or loss of individual identity. Men seem to struggle most with this lost art to masculinity while women appear to come by it naturally (there are exceptions to both). Men need to be more like Esau, who grieved when he lost his birthright. David mourned the death of his blood covenant friend, Jonathan, whom he loved like a relative. Women, this devotion is targeted at encouraging men to dive into the unknown and unlikely–to begin the pursuit of quality relationships with men in an accountable scriptural fashion.

To put it in clear form, I will list the five levels of a relationship, then follow them with barriers to intimacy:

Level 1 is talking about the weather or other vague subjects.

Level 2 is offering an opinion about the weather.

Level 3 is expressing a belief or conviction.

Level 4 is when others share their dreams, fears and emotions with me.

Level 5 is when I share my dreams, fears and emotions with others.

Note: Many men can get to Level 3, but true relationships take place on Levels 4 and 5.

Barriers for men include:

Men don't give each other affection.

Men don't nurture each other.

Men don't talk to each other about intimate things.

Men don't befriend other men just to enjoy their friendship.

Listen up! Before you dive into this unnatural episode you should know that this formula leads to intimacy and includes solid identity, empathy, loyalty, basic trust and delay of gratification. Do yourself a favor and realize that with this type of relationship you'll become vulnerable and Christ-like.

★ ★ ★

FINDING THE REAL ME

*But we all, with unveiled face beholding as in a mirror the glory of the
Lord, are being transformed into the same image from glory
to glory just as from the Lord, the Spirit.*
2 Corinthians 3:18

★ ★ ★

Every time I pick up a magazine or scan the bookstore shelves these days, I find several publications that try (key word in sentence) to decipher the "real" me.

It appears we all give ourselves away psychologically every time we choose Pepsi over Coke or eat cold Wheaties instead of hot Cream of Wheat. One article I read counseled me on how the colors I choose could tell me what sort of mood I was going to be in that day (go figure). Never mind wasting all that time in a shrink's office on a couch, just let someone interpret your wardrobe. I never clued in that maybe wearing a red T-shirt could strip my emotions bare to the world . . . awesome dude! On one of those classy (yeah, right) talk shows the other day, they had as the guest a "mood evaluator" who told the audience you can give your life-long secrets away by what you wear, drive, buy or sell (sounds a little "iffy" to me).

I'm not so sure that this practice of "finding one's self" isn't an age old tradition. The ironic thing is that the book I've been reading (the Bible) tells me to "deny self" in order to find it . . . get it? You know . . . lose to find, die to live, bury to resurrect? Wait a minute—this thinking goes against every concept or theory known to modern man. You will not, I repeat, will not find the "real you" until you get rid of self for the cause of Christ. The "real you," by nature (the sin one), has the capability to murder, lie, cheat, steal, hate, boast . . . need I go on? The Christ in you, after you remove self and replace it with Him, has the capacity to experience real peace, love an enemy, have compassion for the hungry and forgive the unforgivable. Sound like you? No, because it's not the "real you," it's the "transformed you." Now that's one transformation even the crew of the *Starship Enterprise* couldn't figure out.

★ ★ ★

Further Study: What is it that makes us want to find (like it's hiding) the "real me?" Why do you think Jesus wants us to die to self? Why is that process so hard? How can you deny yourself in the next hour? Go do it, okay?

GRADUATION DAY

*Yet you do not know what your life will be like tomorrow. Your life is but
a vapor that appears for a little while and then vanishes away.*
James 4:14

★ ★ ★

Graduation day, whether it be from high school or college, is not only an accomplishment, but for some, a relief. The tougher the studies get, the harder the diploma comes. To set out on this adventure is more than taking a course in math or science. To arrive at the final destination in a gym or auditorium dressed in a cap and gown, lookin' like an ordained minister is exciting. To walk down the aisle in front of beaming parents and gloating in-laws to receive a certificate of graduation evolves into a memorable moment. Realize it or not, this event is a mirror of real life experiences. It starts in elementary school and ends at death. We all go from the bottle, to crawling, to walking, to talking, to riding a bike, to kindergarten, then elementary school, to junior high, onward to high school, to driving, to college, to career, to marriage, to kiddos who call you mommy or daddy, to retirement, then to the life hereafter. That's the question . . . what is the hereafter? It will be the ultimate graduation ceremony we all will be a part of. When does it happen? The book of James says like a vapor or mist. The common world can't predict it nor schedule its arrival time.

How do you handle death when it passes by your house? It may come knocking on the door of a parent, coach, friend or sibling first. It's been said that there are two things we all must do . . . pay taxes and graduate (die). The purpose of this devotion is not to start your day out on a down note, but to get you to thinkin'. Death doesn't have to be sad when you know where you're graduating to. Jesus is the ultimate commencement speaker who holds the certificate of heaven in His, and only His, hands. Do you have family, friends, or others who you know won't be a part of the happy graduation experience? Are you sure that you are ready today, at a moment's notice, to walk the aisle of eternity with Christ? If yes, then your degree is gonna' take you farther than just a career. If not, maybe you should consider what you're graduating into.

★ ★ ★

Further Study: What scares you most about death? Are you sure you're gonna' receive a diploma of life? If not, how can you get on the right course?

KILLER WEEDS

See to it that no one comes short of the grace of God, that no root of bitterness springing up causes trouble, and by it many be defiled.
Hebrews 12:15

★ ★ ★

It was hotter than chili peppers in mid-July. I would make a gentleman's wager that the soles on my sneakers were melting like butter on a hot frying pan. I had this idea (a real brainstorm) which was about as bright as a two-watt lightbulb. How in the world I let my mom talk me and my dad into planting a garden is beyond my capacity to comprehend. I have a new-found respect for the farmers of America who actually enjoy this voyage of vegetation and can make an honest living at it. Now, if you've never had the pain . . . ah, I mean privilege of gathering groceries from the green earth, let my feeble mind take you through the process, one corn row at a time. Okay, I'll go real slow so I don't lose ya' along the way. First, you till the ground under. Second, you plant seeds of whatever your little heart desires to grow. Finally, you water the little suckers. Now, was that tough? (You'll be tested on this Monday.) Oooh, yes, there is one small detail I forgot to tell you about: Weeds can grow up around your vegetables and choke them to death so all that's left are a few hard-as-rock peas.

Now, you must be asking yourself at this point, "Self, what the heck does a garden with weeds have to do with life?" Weeds are like bitterness that left unattended (and not dealt with) can grow up and choke out all the life in your life. Lots of folks carry around the excess baggage of bitterness and it robs all their joy and happiness like a slick shoplifter. The way to deal with bitterness is weed it out–get to the root of the issue and pull it out. In other words, the best way to deal with it is to deal with it! Don't let your garden of life be overtaken with the worldliness of weeds. Communicate, deal with it, root it out and then walk away from it. Make sure you weed your life of bitterness on a daily basis so that you, in due time, will reap a good harvest.

★ ★ ★

Further Study: What is bitterness? How does it spring up in your life? Do you have bitterness toward anyone today? How can you root it out of your life? Are you? When?

GO FIGURE

No one can be my disciple who does not give up all his own possessions.
Luke 14:33

★ ★ ★

It was one of those errand things that sent me into the jaws of the grocery store at rush hour. Granted, most men are banished from these "malls of meals" for the simple reason they haven't a clue what to buy, what aisle to search, or what has any nutritional value. My wife had endured one of those L-O-N-G days with the kids, so I thought (I always get into trouble when I start thinking) I would win the "Husband of the Month" award by volunteering to pick up a few items at the grocery store for her. My motive was good, but this chore would soon turn into a nightmare when I realized (after waiting through the check-out line) that I only had a $20 bill and no checks with me. My calculator mind set immediately into action, figured up the cost of the items in my cart, and guess what? My total was $39.25, which by my calculations, left me in a real pickle of a position—and $19.25 short.

I'll never forget the humiliation as I stood there, trying to seek a quick line of credit in front of a mob of mad mothers. My problem wasn't necessarily bad shopping skills, as much as it was not counting the cost of my purchases. Many Christians today walk around doing what I did—not counting the entire cost of being a disciple of Christ. Jesus figured it up before He took on the job of Savior, and realized it would cost Him His life. In this passage of scripture, Jesus is explaining that a possession is anything that detours you from total commitment to Him. Don't get into the thick of this Christian stuff and then calculate the cost of being a real follower of Christ. Trust me—being short of the cost can bring on a whole lot of embarrassment.

★ ★ ★

Further Study: How much has being a follower of Jesus cost you? What possessions must you give up to be a disciple? Why is Jesus so jealous of all our attention?

CRY BABY

Then all the people (Israelites) *lifted up their voices
and cried, and the people wept all night.*
Numbers 14:1

★ ★ ★

I remember learning in a high school health class how good crying is for us. It serves many purposes such as relieving stress, washing out foreign debris from the eye socket and unclogging the tear ducts of babies and probably adults, too. No matter how tough someone may seem, we all have cried at some point or another in our lives. Crying can be a part of a mourning process after the loss of a loved one, or a reaction from lack of sleep, or a release of too much stress. Whatever the cause, crying is a God-made way of dealing or coping in life.

Moses and Joshua dealt with a different kind of crying as they led a whole mess of people (Israelites) out of slavery, across the desert and through the Red Sea (sounds like over the river and through the woods to grandmother's house we go), and put up with a whole bunch of whining. This crying (whining) didn't stem from pure motives or sincere faith, but the lack of both of these. You see, this is a great example of how not all expressed emotion such as crying and weeping is sincere. At times, people shed tears that are not valid. Some moments you can see that the tears are of anger or lack of faith (God failed them), and they are wrong. Don't take a God-given emotion and use it as a mortal manipulation. You can see in this example that God allowed these people to wander in the wilderness until all of them died off because they were wrong in their ways. Go ahead, cry all you want to; just make sure it's not a fake.

★ ★ ★

Further Study: When was the last time you cried? What caused it? How did you solve the situation that provoked it, or did you? Have you ever cried insincere tears? Why?

SECOND WIND

Do all your work heartily for the Lord rather than for men.
Colossians 3:23

★ ★ ★

It was a hot August day, and I happened to be wearing a hot football uniform under the guidance of a hot-tempered coach. These three did not go well for my health during two-a-day workouts preparing for the coming season. I remember how that day's practice schedule went about as slowly as a duck swimming in oil. It dragged on and on and on until I heard my coach say, "Boys, everyone on the line for some pukers." Sorry for the graphic language, but that meant we now had to run sprints until we dropped. I felt like this would be the perfect time to get run over by a steamroller, just to extinguish my pain. I was on the line ready to drop when out of the corner of my helmet, between the face guard bars, I saw . . . beauty in the bleachers. Yep, my girlfriend had come to watch her sugar plum, sweetie pie, honey muffin practice. Hot dog, did I perk up, pooch out my chest, stand up tall and begin to clap and cheer up my teammates who were ready for a stretcher. It was like a second wind (maybe just puppy love) came over me, and you'd think I'd been shot out of a cannon the way I ran those sprints. Miracles still happen.

We are a people who are in the "do" mode most of the time. We go, go, go like a hamster on a treadmill, day in and day out. We work, serve, slave throughout our lives, but for whom? Are we trying to earn our ticket aboard the heavenly Airways Express? To do whatever we're doing for our Creator rather than a crowd will take a new perspective, since we live in a world that bases acceptance on performance. God is more than happy to help in this process that starts in a prayer. Give God your glory, and see if your reward isn't relished more. Imagine God in the bleachers, cheering you on in your daily tasks, and see if you don't find a second wind.

★ ★ ★

Further Study: Do you do all you do for you, or who? What kind of work do you do daily? How can you give the glory to God?

45

FESS UP

*Then the King said to him, "How many times must I tell you to speak
to me nothing but the truth in the name of the Lord?"*
2 Chronicles 18:15

★ ★ ★

One of the favorite pastimes at our ranch while growing up was to
shoot water moccasin snakes in our pond. They were a hazard to our bull-
frog population, not to mention they could bite the fire out of ya'. These
slithery, slimy, scum surviving snakes were best seen sunning on the shore
on a hot summer's day (say that sentence fast 10 times). We would drive
our tractor to the edge of the bank, raise up the bucket full of friends, guns
and plenty of ammo to its full extension for maximum viewing, then commence to firing away at will. One day, our routine snake hunt turned into
an unplanned nightmare. We accidentally drove the $40,000 tractor into
the pond. Man, oh man, did I know that I was gonna' get it. My dad was-
n't with us; in fact, no parent was, and we all knew if he found out, we
would all hang at high noon. We got a neighboring farmer to pull out the
submerged submarine, cleaned it up, raked the tire tracks leading into the
pond and got it running again by 2:00 a.m.

How many times have you been in a pure pickle that you knew would
spell out pure trouble? The real question is, did you ever get away with it
scot-free? Did you lie or just not tell at all? How characteristic that in story
after story we see biblical characters doing the same? You know, hey . . .
what they don't know can't hurt them, or one white lie never killed anyone. The problem comes when we start small and it becomes a common
routine in our lives. God, whether you know it or will admit it, is everywhere at once and is all knowing. He sees deceit, cheating, lying, stealing,
hating and defiling even when common folks don't. He is faithful and just
to forgive us of these, yet we are called also to make it right with the per-
son(s) we victimized. Keeping a clean slate is tough, yet our conscience is
relieved when we do. I know you're wondering what I did. Yes, I did con-
ceal the truth, and yes, my dad did find out. How? . . . (suspense is building isn't it?) the neighbor told him and yes, I did get it!

★ ★ ★

Further Study: When was the last time you lied? Did you confess or con-
ceal? How will you handle it differently next time?

MENTOR ME

*And the things which you've received from me, entrust these
to faithful men who can teach others also.*
2 Timothy 2:2

★ ★ ★

Let me set the scene, 1988, 4 X 100 relay in the Summer Olympics equipped with a peerless group of sprint champions, and it was inconceivable that the United States team could lose the gold medal. Yet, as the final leg of the relay approached, the unbelievable happened. The Americans dropped the baton, the crowd moments earlier electrified, became mute.

This disastrous scene aptly describes the essence of loss that "Generation X" feels as they enter adulthood. Searching desperately for godly mentors to teach and model, they feel like runners stranded at the starting blocks with no baton. Our country is teeming with young men and women who have little identity or direction, missing a sense of continuity with our heritage. This fact underscores our need for mature, growing older men and women to pull up along side these young folks and hand off the baton of godliness and leadership to equip the next generation. Mentoring is a relational experience through which one person empowers another by sharing God-given resources. The resources will vary but mentoring is a positive dynamic that enables people to develop their potential. Observing someone's growth, struggles, responses and decision-making process can change the perspective of a mentoree forever. Mentoring can reduce the probability of leadership failure, divorce, provide accountability and empower a responsible, potential laborer. Mentoring is as old as civilization itself. The Old Testament showed this with Eli and Samuel, Elijah and Elisha, Barnabas and Paul. These days the human touch has been replaced with computers, videos, books and classrooms.

Many years ago my wife and I began taking young men and women into our home to live for a year. Yes, it's like living your life in a fish bowl and demands a higher energy level, but the rewards will be eternal. These folks become a part of our family, and we don't even realize how profound our words and actions really are. People were and still are God's method for making disciples. The self-made man or woman is a myth and, though some claim it, few aspire to it. You, yes you, have what it takes to mentor if you see potential in others, are flexible, patient, and are experiencing continuing growth toward holiness. If you're willing . . . there's someone out there waiting to receive the baton and continue the race; don't drop it.

★ ★ ★

Further Study: Who could you mentor?

Personal Touch

Let the one who is taught the word share all good things with him who teaches.
Galatians 6:6

★ ★ ★

One of the all-time greatest on the gridiron is a guy named Jerry Rice. He plays for the San Francisco 49ers' football team and is considered by most experts the best wide receiver in the history of the NFL. Once, Jerry was asked why he attended such a small, obscure university like Mississippi Valley State University in Itta Bena, Mississippi. Jerry's response was, "Out of all the big-time schools (like UCLA) that recruited me, MVSU was the only school to come to my house for a personal visit." The big-time powerhouse universities send out generic letters, cards and advertisements, but only this one showed Rice personal attention and sincere concern.

When I heard this story it brought to mind just how important personal outreach is. Here is a guy who few thought valuable enough to recruit personally, but now he's a superstar in the sports world. Gang, people, no matter what color or size or nationality, are valuable. How much more important is the personal touch in matters concerning the heart, soul and spirit of a person. If you're in the business market and you don't extend a personal touch to your clients, then get ready to go belly-up (broke). Wal-Mart would not be the nation's number one discount center without friendly smiles, warm handshakes, (low prices) and personal demeanor. Every Wal-Mart store in America has a greeter at the door to offer you their services. Christians need to learn from old "Wally World" and make evangelism personal and more practical. Each person you meet deserves your personal best, not your bulk mail worst. Do God, and yourself, a favor and put a personal touch into your outreach formula.

★ ★ ★

Further Study: Are you giving your best? Do you have a tendency to be generic instead of personal in sharing with others? How valuable do you see those who are different from you?

48

THREE SIMPLE WORDS

Love never fails.
1 Corinthians 13:8

★ ★ ★

February 14 is Valentine's Day, a time set aside for lovers of all ages. This day for romanticism was created, no doubt, by florists, candy makers and greeting card companies. Businesses rake in big-time cash simply by offering folks a creative way to say, "I love you," at that special time each year. Despite the hoopla and commercialization, I think Valentine's Day is a great idea, and the male species needs all the help it can get. Perhaps you're asking yourself why I've included a valentine devotion on February 13 rather than February 14. Why? Because it is never too late or too early to tell someone you love them. Love is the high octane fuel that powers our engine and keeps us going. Relationships, whether with the opposite sex or not, need to be nurtured so they don't wither like a plant without water.

Unfortunately, millions of marriages, friendships and working relationships are in trouble today because of the inability of those involved to get along. Maybe the fundamental problem is selfishness. We are so intent on satisfying our own needs and desires that we fail to recognize the longings of others. Relationships always work best when we think less about ourselves and more about another. True agape (unconditional) love is hardly a new concept. In fact, it's ancient. Jesus not only told us, He modeled for us, the way to develop, build, nurture and sustain a valuable relationship. Whatever our height, weight, color, or shoe-size, we all have two basic needs–to love and be loved by someone. Begin today to humble yourself (even if you've been wronged) and mend an old relationship, work to maintain a current one, or develop a brand new relationship. Make Jesus the real cupid, a model for what it really takes, and what it really means to say three simple words–I . . . love   . . . you!

★ ★ ★

Further Study: What does love mean to you? Why is it so hard to maintain a relationship? How are you nurturing your relationships today?

VALENTINE'S DAY

Love is patient; love is kind, is not jealous, does not brag, isn't arrogant,
doesn't act unbecomingly, does not seek its own, is not provoked,
doesn't take into account a wrong suffered, doesn't rejoice in
unrighteousness, but rejoices in truth, bears all things,
believes all things, hopes all things, endures
all things. Love never fails.
1 Corinthians 13:4-8

★ ★ ★

There aren't many typical days lived experiencing the love which is exchanged on this day. Cupid starts firing arrows in the direction of our tender hearts, moving us to share this day with someone we love. The card shops, flower nurseries and candy stores make a killing each year on this day. It seems like the collars tighten up around the male sex to first, not forget February 14th, but even more impressive, to try out those creative skills and come up with a day she won't soon forget. I'm no expert on understanding the opposite sex, but I have learned that it's the little things that really matter. You don't have to be married or have a relationship going on to have a sweetheart. It could be that a sister, mom or another female relative falls into the category of a valentine. The cards are cute, the flowers are favorites and the candy dandy, but Valentine's Day is love God's way.

When you read what Paul wrote to the church in Corinth, he defines what we should be wrapping up in our actions to give to our sweeties. This love is a written description of what God's true love is to you as a child of God. God celebrates this special day year-round. Do you know how people would view you if you really took to heart (pun) these verses in your life daily? Give a gift today that won't wilt without water, that doesn't melt under heat, or end up in a scrapbook. That gift is applied scripture. Look out cupid, this is one arrow that shoots long and deep into our hearts.

★ ★ ★

Further Study: What ways can you show your sweetheart you really value him/her?

50

EMPATHY

Carry each other's burdens, and in this way you will fulfill the law of Christ.
Galatians 6:2

★ ★ ★

Mr. Alter's fifth grade class at Lake Elementary School in Oceanside, California, included 14 bald-headed boys. Only one had no choice in the matter. Ian O'Gorman was losing his hair in clumps as the result of the chemotherapy used to fight lymphoma. So Ian wouldn't feel out of place in the classroom, all 13 of his buddies shaved their heads, too. If they all were bald, no one could point out the one who had cancer. A 10-year-old boy named Kyle started it all as he proposed the plan to the group, then marched them all down to the barber. Ian's father, touched by the gesture of compassion, was in tears as he told them how he appreciated their kindness and good deed.

What an awesome example of carrying a burden for a friend. You don't often see such a sense of compassion. Take a look sometime at the words that precede an act of healing by Jesus in the gospels. They state, "He felt compassion, so . . .." So what? Sew buttons on your underwear? No. So, He did something about it by expressing empathy for the afflicted and became part of the solution, not the problem. There is probably no better way to show how much Jesus you have living in your heart than by carrying someone else's burden(s). Our second greatest commandment is, "Love your neighbor as yourself." Do you realize just how much you love yourself? Let me answer that, and I don't even know you . . . a lot! Tune in to the spirit of Christ and see where He leads you and what cross (burden) He leads you to carry for a friend. You'll feel good about yourself, and this selfish world will know that you are different.

★ ★ ★

Further Study: How compassionate are you? Have you ever acted on that sense? Why or why not? Who could you help today? What are you waiting on?

LANDING LEADERS

Let not many of you be leaders because you know that
we who lead will be judged more strictly.
James 3:1

★ ★ ★

Flight No. 401 on Eastern Airlines was making a routine approach at the Los Angeles airport. Throughout the journey there had been little or no turbulence and preparations were being made for landing. The crew was made up of five stewardesses, a captain, first assistant and a flight navigator. After making final contact with the tower in L.A. and being cleared for landing, the captain flipped the switch to engage the landing gear and noticed that the indicator light didn't come on. The crew did a quick visual check and found the landing gear was down, which indicated that the light itself must be burned out. To make sure that the bulb was the problem, the plane continued to circle the airport while the navigator tried to remove the bulb from the instrument panel, but couldn't. The first assistant also tried, then the captain. Little did they realize that while the entire cabin crew was messing with one little bulb, the plane was losing altitude and ultimately crashed in a swampy area miles from the airport, killing hundreds. This tragedy was caused by a bulb valued at 75 cents. That's right . . . a cheap bulb was the root cause of a multi-million dollar plane crash that cost hundreds of lives. Why? Because the captain took his eyes off the big picture, his main responsibility, to deal with a meaningless job of no value.

We, as leaders, need to keep flying the plane, not dabbling with dinkies. As a leader you must maintain a focus on what really matters or what doesn't at the time of decision making. We need to learn to "choose our mountains" to climb in life. There is always gonna' be tons of stuff to do, events to volunteer for, committees to serve on and meetings to attend, but there are really only 24 hours in a day (that I can tell). Learn to see (through God's eyes) what is a priority and what can wait. Learn to say no to some things and guard your time with your family and God. Learn to delegate to others so they can learn and you just take the priority lists. Leadership isn't a title, it's a learned skill.

★ ★ ★

Further Study: Who is the best Christian leader you've ever seen at work? What made them so good at leading others? How can you be an effective leader? How do you learn to prioritize?

A TONGUE LASHING

They set their mouth against the heavens and
their tongue parades loose through the earth.
Psalm 73:9

✱ ✱ ✱

Take a look at the human anatomy for a moment. Look specifically at the head (neck up). Have you noticed that we all have two ears, a mouth and one nose (I hope)? Do you see that you can close and open the mouth but not the ears? Why? Do you think it's just an assembly line mistake and God is soon to have a factory recall on everyone's face any day now? Growing up, I'm sure you hummed the tune of "sticks and stones may break my bones, but words can never hurt me." I bet the guy who wrote that must have been a hermit in a cave on a deserted island to have made up such a lie. Untruthful words can probably do more damage to a person than diving into an empty pool. The tongue has done more damage to the human race than the black plague or polio. With it we praise our friends then turn around and stab them in their backs. Why, oh why?

The Bible says the tongue is the bit in a horse's mouth, the spark that sets off a forest fire and the poison of a cobra. To realize its power one must first realize its whereabouts and where it hides . . . in your mouth. Self-image, reputation and potential can be all but destroyed by a few words of gossip. What defines the word gossip? Speaking to anyone about another person's business that is neither part of the solution or problem. It's trying to knock someone down a notch for selfish reasons. This is why God tells us to be quick to listen and slow to speak. Today's galloping gossips seem to have this verse flipped around. Learn to tame your tongue and put out rumors when they come to you; don't fuel their fire. Listen to yourself in a conversation with others and see if you're spreading a rumor, or stating a fact or fiction. Do yourself and others a favor by being a different breed of person and not letting that muscle in your mouth exercise on someone else's life.

✱ ✱ ✱

Further Study: Do you gossip? Do you say things to others in order to demean someone else? How can you begin to tame your tongue? How can you train it to speak the truth?

53

STOOPING

But God demonstrates his own love for us in this:
while we were yet sinners, Christ died for us.
Romans 5:8

★ ★ ★

A vivid picture exists in my brain of a ritual which seems to take place annually in March. If you know anything about horses or horse breeding, you know that March is the "foal" time of the year. That's the time when pregnant mares have their colts out in pastures on ranches across the south. There is nothing quite like seeing a newborn colt trying with all its four-legged might to stand up and walk for the first time. It's amazing how soon after birth and the mom licking the colt clean that it learns to maneuver. I remember my dad, upon sight of a newborn colt in one of his pastures, crawling for up to a half mile on his hands and knees toward the mare and colt. It's the first time the colt would have ever seen a human before and should be scared, but it's not. The fact that with no rope or halter or feed bucket, my father could stoop up to this colt and begin to rub its legs, back, belly, and head without scaring it is amazing. The key element to this is never allowing your head to be taller than the colt's head.

The Hebrew meaning of the word "grace" is to stoop or bow. Have you ever realized that the Creator of this world crawls to you for miles (humbly) and comes to you to get to know you? (Remember, He humbled Himself.) Listen . . . God could have walked up to you all proud and tough, but He knew you would run (like the colt) if He did. Remember, He knocks gently at the door to our hearts; He doesn't kick it down (Revelation 3:20). What a unique sight it was to see my dad humble himself to a horse to get to know it, but what an awesome picture it is to see the God who holds each star in place crawl to us in order to save us from eternal death.

★ ★ ★

Further Study: What does grace mean to you? How have you seen God humble Himself or stoop in your life? How did you respond? What does grace do to you and for your relationship to Christ?

DON'T SWEAT THE SMALL STUFF

Yes, woe upon you, Pharisees, and you other religious leaders–hypocrites!
For you tithe down to the last mint leaf in your garden, but ignore
the important things–justice and mercy and faith. Yes, you
should tithe, but you shouldn't leave the more
important things undone . . . You strain
out a gnat and swallow a camel.
Matthew 23:23-24

★ ★ ★

As a child on my grandparents' farm, I spent time "putting by" (as the farm folks say). "Putting by" means preserving farm produce so it can be stored to use later. The method of the day was canning. My grandma was good at it. She canned everything, but my favorite was jelly.

We were so proud of the jelly we entered it in the fair one year, sure the judges would agree it was worth the effort it took to produce. But victory was not ours. A piece of peel had made it through the strainer and got wedged between the judge's teeth, so the prize went to someone who had made jelly from commercial grape juice, smooth and peel-less, but not "homemade."

Often in life we struggle so with insignificant (in the context of eternity) blips that we completely miss the genuine intent, then turn our backs and let a humongous injustice stomp right past us. Just prior to this verse Jesus spoke to the crowds concerning Jewish law in Jerusalem, after He'd booted the money changers out of the Temple. Angry at His acceptance from the crowd, the Pharisees tried to trip up Jesus with trick questions about God's laws.

If we're constantly searching for the smallest flaw, the least mistake, the one place where we colored outside the lines, we're liable to miss the grand design, the big picture (catchin' on?). Jesus said that if you follow the first and greatest commandment to love the Lord your God with all your heart, soul, and mind, you'll find you are obeying all the others (Matthew 23:37-40). Keep Jesus in your heart, your eyes on God and don't sweat the small stuff. Gnats go down a lot easier than camels . . . one hump, or two?

★ ★ ★

Further Study: What chokes you that really is insignificant in the light of eternity? Why?

GIFT OF GIVING

When He (Jesus) *ascended into heaven, He led captive a host of captives and, He gave gifts to men* (women).
Ephesians 4:8

★ ★ ★

You're gonna' love this devotion if you're one of those who wakes up early and runs with happy feet downstairs before dawn to open up presents on Christmas and to see if Santa stuffed your stocking. One of the greatest seasons we have on this planet is the celebration season of Jesus' birth when we get presents, too. When was the last time you went to someone's birthday party and received more goodies than the birthday boy or girl? (Party favors don't count). If and when you have children, you will know what I'm talking about when I say the kiddos get "excited!" If you're not planning to get married, you can relate because you were a child once. Christmas and all the festive frenzies that go along with this spirit are too few and far between. Wouldn't it be great to have this celebration of joy when everyone's happy, caring and full of turkey, each month? I'll take that idea back because I'd be broke and weigh two tons if we did. So record over that message, will ya'? Jesus really is the reason for this spectacular season, and isn't it fun to be invited each year? There's nothing quite like giving and receiving fun things.

Jesus really does, through His Spirit, allow us to open gifts. His gifts. He has graciously given some to you (with no take-backs) to enjoy daily. What gifts am I speaking of? Spiritual gifts. In His family room He leaves, nicely wrapped for you to open and use daily, divine gifts for His glory. Your present may be the gift of giving, so give. The gift of mercy, so care. The gift of teaching, so train. The gift of exhortation, so encourage, or the gift of discernment, so choose. Whatever you find under God's giving tree, open it, use it, and be thankful. These gifts are like the EverReady Bunny . . . they keep going and going and going.

★ ★ ★

Further Study: Do you open up your divine spiritual gift daily? Why or why not? How can you use it today?

A Standard of Quality

*In those days Israel had no king, and everyone did
what was right in their own eyes.*
Judges 21:25

★ ★ ★

The sport of track is one of history prior. It is amazing how endurance, speed and quickness play such a pivotal role in this competition between individuals. It is one of these sports that at the end of the race, you can't blame coming in last on another teammate for missing the shot, fumbling the ball, duffing a serve or whiffing a pitch. As this sport evolved, new events were added to enhance the viewing and generate some flare for the public and the participants. The event . . . high jumping. I ask you, who would be creative enough (if that's what you'd call it) to come up with a sport where a person bounces over a bar, Fosbury Flops and then pile drives themselves into a pit? Have you ever noticed that the way the winner is determined is by the continual movement of the bar up in height and the weeding out process of the jumpers not being able to jump over the advancing bar? What would happen if the bar wasn't needed and everyone was scored by their own standard? Talk about chaos, talk about disagreements. The bar is the standard which the participants have to shoot (jump) for in order to test themselves. As the bar moves up, the standard to conquer becomes more difficult to achieve, yet more rewarding to attain.

Can you imagine a world without a standard and a society without a Savior? You should, you're living in one as we speak. Our society seems to have drifted onto the rocks of destruction without notice. The Bible is full of past civilizations who seem to have come up with their own rules and ended up failing the test. Jesus is our standard, our world record holder, our model of excellence we are shooting for. Without Him going before us setting the scale, walking beside us, helping us compete, following us up, and holding us accountable, we wouldn't make it. Don't get mad at the standard. It's there for you to shoot for. Never lose hope in the King, He's the record holder. So what are you waiting on? It's your jump next!

★ ★ ★

Further Study: How much do you prepare daily for attaining His standard? How much did you prepare today? (If not, then get after it!)

STEPPIN' OUT

And He said, "Come" and Peter stepped out of the boat and
walked on the water and came toward Jesus.
Matthew 14:29

★ ★ ★

Have you ever been summoned to step out before? How about at a track meet when the coach tells you, before the final race, to step out? What about when a friend encourages you to step out of your comfort zone and try something different? How about on the dance floor? When does someone describes you as steppin' out of your normal ways and doing something totally out of character?

I love the story of Peter (the disciple) being scared from sailing in the storm. He looked off the port side (just a guess) and saw someone apparently walking on top of the rough seas. He rubbed his red eyes and did a double take. It was at that moment he realized it was his hero, Jesus, and then he was asked to come along for a casual walk on the water. Sure! Right! Can't you just hear old Pete saying to himself, "Jesus, you must be crazy . . . me, walk on that water? I don't think so."

The ending to this scene in scripture is worth reading again. Peter, Mr. Aggressive, jumped out of the boat (his comfort zone) and began walking on the water toward Jesus. He must have felt pretty powerful and cool until that moment he took his focus off Christ. Reality set in, and when he looked down, he began to sink like a brick. I'm not sure about this, but I'll bet ya' that Peter was no All-American swimmer and wondered if he wasn't about to become shark bait.

Jesus calls us daily to walk away from security blankets and step out in faith to follow Him. Walking on water is not easy, but neither is having total faith in the Master's plans. Faith is the assurance of things hoped for (fear of not drowning) and the conviction of things not seen (waves of turbulent tough times). Go ahead . . . step out. Jesus won't let you sink.

★ ★ ★

Further Study: Has God ever called you to step out of your comfort zone and do something totally radical for Him? Why is it so tough to step out on unsure waters and follow him? When will you step out of your boat?

CONFIDENCE CREATOR

And Elijah answered and said, "If I am a man of God, let fire come down from heaven and consume you and your fifty." Then the fire of God came down from heaven and consumed him and his fifty.

2 Kings 1:12

★ ★ ★

Confidence is something to be compared with bravery in a war. Some call it reliance, assurance, certainty and faith, but scripture calls it faith, trust, hope, conviction, belief and dependence. My father used to tell me, "If your ability was half of your confidence, you'd be dangerous." The problem we humans seem to have with confidence is that we have it in the wrong things. We tend to put all our cards on our business brains, athletic attributes, luxurious looks or witty way with words. This is why so many have such low self-image–because we fail in areas that we rely on self, not God, to be successful.

Elijah, as you probably know, was a great prophet. He was called upon by God to be a communicator and public address system of the truths to come. He was obedient to his calling which allowed him to have divine confidence that his Master's messages would not be mocked and would "hold water," so to speak, when tested. Elijah had the confidence (faith) that when he picked up the phone to call upon the Creator, he would not get a busy signal. What trust it must have taken to stand in front of a bunch of doubting dummies and put his God (the Almighty) to the test. It was kinda like a youngster saying, "My dad can beat up your dad." God the Father has not, nor will He ever be made out to be a joke (mocked). Elijah called down the fire from heaven, and at once (not a moment's notice) his wish came true in full force. You see, God doesn't do anything halfway, and this includes showing His power over a false god. Learn from this and know that you worship this same God who shows Himself the all powerful, yet knows how many hairs you have on your head. Have your confidence (faith) in the right thing, not things. Remember, they will someday all burn.

★ ★ ★

Further Study: Where does your confidence come from? How confident are you in the flesh? Is God the power in your strength?

DISGUISED

In order that no advantage be taken of us by Satan,
for we are not ignorant of his schemes (disguises).
2 Corinthians 2:11

★ ★ ★

One of my favorite friends also happens to be a big animal lover. He has four children who know their father has a soft spot for critters. On one occasion, he caught a baby raccoon and brought it home for the kids to see. At a family dinner meeting that night, they came up with a name for the new arrival–"Bandit." One fact about raccoons they seemed to overlook is that as they mature, these animals go through a glandular change and often become aggressive to the point of attack. Since a 30-pound raccoon can equal a 100 pound dog in a fight, they can be the source of extensive hospital bills. I recall talking to the nine-year-old daughter about the dilemma, and her response was, "Bandit wouldn't hurt me . . . he just wouldn't!" But, after several friends of the family and their own kids suffered puncture wounds and face lacerations, they released the beast back to the wilderness.

I'm reminded how sin often comes disguised (dressed) in an adorable appearance, and as we play, it becomes easy to say, "It will be different for me," but the result of this type thinking is predictable. Sin is like fire–if you mess with it, you will get burned. Don't be taken in (lured) by Satan's appearance as a harmless creature, but be wise to his power and schemes to destroy you . . . the wounds can be fatal!

★ ★ ★

Further Study: Are you deceived by sin's disguise? Do you ever think you are superman or superwoman, capable of taking on sin? How can you wise up to sin's game?

NO GUTS, NO GLORY

*The proof of your faith, being more precious than gold which is
perishable, even though tested by fire, may be found to
result in praise, glory and honor to Christ.*
1 Peter 1:7

✫ ✫ ✫

Close your eyes (no dozing off now) and say to yourself the title of
this devotion and see what visions dance in your head. No fair seeing sugar
plums either. This kind of line is called "baiting" if you want to know the
street name for it. You use this "one-liner" when you want to coax, or per-
suade, someone to do something they probably wouldn't do on their own.
It's kind of a "guts" check on the spot, you might say. You'll hear it on the
ski slopes, on the 20 foot bluffs of a lake, in the athletic arenas and at the
late night parties. Sometimes it's a sincere effort to motivate, and other
times it's to set someone up for failure or destruction. No matter where you
call home, or what your age is, this phrase chooses no favorites and knows
not of the consequences.

You hear this lingo in the secular world more than you will in the
Christian circles. I offer you a suggestion. We need to hear it more on the
God Squad, too. Isn't it true we are athletes, warriors, risk takers in this for-
given family? Are we not called to run in such a way that we may win!?
Doesn't it take guts to receive the crown of eternal life called heaven? You
bet your sweet potatoes it does! This Christian stuff is no walk through the
lily fields or a yellow brick road (sorry Dorothy). Folks without guts in this
league (Christianity) won't last too long. I would much rather be considered a risk taker in my faith, than a bench sitter. It's a heck of a lot better
to have tried and failed, than never to have tried at all. Failure helps us realize that we are human and we do need a Savior. Step up to the plate and
take a 100 percent swing. Remember, home runs in this league are always
preceded by a few strikeouts, but that makes the successes for Christ all the
more to celebrate about. Have some guts and see some glory. Go God's
way.

✫ ✫ ✫

Further Study: Why do you shy away from uncertain situations in your
faith? How can you have God's guts?

PERFECT PRACTICE

The goal of our instruction is first love from a pure heart,
good conscience and sincere faith.
1 Timothy 1:5

★ ★ ★

There is a famous NBA basketball star who played for the Boston
Celtics throughout the '80s. His name is Larry Bird. He was a star forward
for Indiana State and fueled his college team to the 1979 NCAA National
Championship showdown with none other than Michigan State, whose
star was Magic Johnson. Larry then went on to a star-studded, all-star
career with the Celtics and led them to several world championships in the
late '80s. The story is told of a pre-game warm-up session in which Larry
was alone, shooting baskets at the Boston Garden a few hours prior to a
playoff game with the L.A. Lakers. After shooting several shots and missing all of them, Larry called upon the arena manager to check to see if the
basket was at the standard height of 10 feet. The arena manager, proud of
his dependability for doing things right the first time, was disgusted with
Larry's questioning his capabilities, but measured the basket a second time.
Much to his surprise, the basket was a half-inch low (hence the reason for
the missed shots).

The point of this story is to show you the importance of knowing
exactly what the goal is that you're shooting for. Larry Bird's goal was a
circle of metal attached to a glass backboard 10 feet from the floor. Our
goal as a Christian is to love others with a healthy heart, a clean conscience
and a flawless faith. We, too, should know in our spirits when the goal is a
bit off and we are probably missing our mark. To love others is not only to
share Jesus with them, but to follow up with discipleship. In other words,
you will be striving after this goal for the rest of your life so don't expect
to stop anytime soon. Larry Bird didn't get all his recognition and rewards
in the sport of basketball by missing his mark often. Christians likewise
don't see the fruits of their labor by failing to follow through with specific
instructions. Perfect practice makes perfect. Hey, and in the end, we'll all
be all-stars in heaven!

★ ★ ★

Further Study: How does this scripture apply to your daily life? What
makes athletes good at what they do? How does that differ from what
allows Christians to excel in their faith? Do you know your exact goals as
a believer? Where are the measurements found? (Hint: the Bible)

FLEET OF FEET

Therefore, since we have so great a cloud of witnesses surrounding us, let us also lay aside every encumbrance and the sin which so easily entangles us, and let us run with endurance the race that is set before us.
Hebrews 12:1

★ ★ ★

If you go to many track meets or cross country events, you will find competitors who are basically made up of only two body parts . . . legs and lungs. My hat is off to those courageous souls who brave the weather and the big neighborhood dogs running loose, to call themselves runners. America is full of pavement beaters who rise up from slumber daily to get the old ticker (heart) in shape for those later years of life. I, for one, standing 6 feet 5 inches tall, weighing in at 220 pounds and accompanied with a flat size thirteen fleet of feet, am not one of that species. When I run, it sounds like a wild herd of elephants escaping from the city zoo and stampeding loose on the streets.

The Bible, over and over, uses the words run and race. The Christian life is compared with a race and the Christian person with a runner who can enter as a participant because of Christ's payment at the cross. The author of Hebrews tells us that in order to succeed in this event, we need to throw off two things: every encumbrance and the sin that trips us up. The sin, in this context, is lack of faith, and the encumbrance is defined as excess weight. In other words, to finish you need faith in God's way and prior training that will allow the weight of worldliness to be burned off like calories.

How are you training today to be a competitive runner for God? How deep is your faith in your Savior, that this race is the most important race of your life? Do yourself a favor and get training for this one because the reward you will receive beats the heck out of any medal or trophy earned today.

★ ★ ★

Further Study: What worldly weight are you carrying with you? How can you lose it?

DAILY PHONE CALLS

As Jesus approached the town gate, a dead person was being carried out, the only son of his mother, and she was a widow. And a large crowd from the town was with her. When Jesus saw her, his heart went out to her, and he felt compassion, and he said, "Don't cry."
Luke 7:12-13

★ ★ ★

On March 12, 1994, I received a phone call while in Telluride, Colorado, that won't quit ringing in my mind for a long time. The call was from my wife, to inform me of a very close friend of mine who died of a heart attack in Houston, Texas. Wow . . . did this news stop me in my tracks. It was weird how I almost didn't seem to believe her (my own wife) and continued to interrogate her on the validity of the news. Death comes so quickly, yet it doesn't play favorites or give much warning of its arrival time. Throughout the entire funeral I noticed the joy on the some fifteen hundred faces attending. It was like those in attendance weren't as concerned with the loss of a friend as they were with the future of the hope. The tears came from loss of a friend, not from having to guess where he had gone. They knew . . . heaven.

If you notice in the scripture, Jesus tells the mother of the deceased son not to cry. Why? Doesn't that seem a little harsh to stomach? After all, He had just stated that He felt compassion for her, right? I believe the reason for this statement by the Savior was because He was in total control. Have you ever noticed the ones who don't get tangled up in the turbulence of the times are those with a heavenly perspective? Remember, the vantage point which overlooks situations from above can be yours also. Now I'm not saying that crying is wrong, and neither is God, as long as your heart realizes that Jesus cares for you and your situations and He holds the future. Hey, it's not bad having a Savior who exemplifies compassion and knowing my friend is residing with his Creator . . . what a set up!

★ ★ ★

Further Study: If you were to lose a friend today, how would you react? How does this scripture apply today?

64

THE TESTING TREE

And God saw all that He had made, and behold it was very good.
Genesis 1:31

✩ ✩ ✩

Picture the most beautiful place you've ever been or seen. Can it even compare with the first place ever created? The Ultimate Artist put His brush and paint to the sky and to the water and to the ground, and at the mention of a word the most exquisite place was formed. My four year old will look at a sunset and say, "Mommy, God painted that."

But what about this perfect garden . . . what was so special? Larry Norman, one of the early rock'n'roll Christians, says in one of his songs, "So long ago the garden." What is his point? I think he means the garden is a place in which we all long to live. No ugliness, no perversion, only complete perfection with purposeful fulfillment. One man, one woman . . . each obviously made for the other.

Isn't it odd that God would have put a very unique tree in that perfect place? My nephew, when at church, was asked, "What was the name of the tree that God forbid Adam and Eve to partake of?" He answered, "The testing tree." It was exactly that, a tree that tested Adam and Eve. They did not do very well on that test, but what would we have done on the very same test? Today we are still trying to reverse the curse of that test. No work for men, easy money, no pain in childbirth and no consequences for our sins.

Well, the ending of that story can be found in Genesis, and it is still happening today. The fact is, until Jesus comes back and we all return to heaven, we will never be in a perfect place with perfect people. But God has given us good instruction and promises concerning what to do until that time occurs. Put His Word to the test . . . .. Love when it hurts to love, heap burning coals and remember . . . He will never leave or forsake us, and He will never give us more than we can handle.

✩ ✩ ✩

Further Study: How have you tried to reverse the curse? What place or person do you wish was perfect? Not one of us is perfect, so how do we handle imperfect people and places?

RED CARPET TREATMENT

But if you show favoritism, you are committing sin
and are convicted by the law as transgressors.
James 2:10

★ ★ ★

A couple of snow-to-snows ago (that's American Indian talk for "years"), I had the opportunity to see the President of the United States, George Bush, when he came for a campaign speech at a local theme park. Talk about an event of the century! Talk about rolling out the red carpet for someone! Oh my! I could not believe what a big to-do it was just for a guy to talk to a few thousand folks. Streets were blocked off for miles, Secret Service agents swarmed like bees, a fleet of limos cruised in, and presidential helicopters filled the airways like a flock of geese. Come on, I mean how many folks does it take to protect one guy, and how can the President fly in all those "copters" at once? (Split personality, maybe?) I was amazed at how people from all around the community basically laid down everything to be of service to a guy who would make a speech, then jet set off to four other cities to repeat this brouhaha again.

We seem to live in a world that will only roll out the red carpet to those who are in high places. We idolize politicians, doctors, lawyers, movie stars and athletes, but seldom do you see someone ask the grocery store bagger for an autograph. The reason, a lot of times, that we play favorites is in hopes we will get a perk, a bonus, a break, a loan from our efforts. God doesn't show favorites in whom He loves and whom He doesn't, does He? Can you imagine a Savior who would only die for those who would pay Him back later? Our light shines brighter when we treat everyone the same–the class clown or the superstar. It's not hard to treat the gifted with special effort, but how about those who aren't the socially accepted types? Then you need God's help. Come on, take a gamble and treat the peons like a president.

★ ★ ★

Further Study: Find someone who'd never expect it, and roll out the red carpet for them today. How does it feel to love the unloved?

ANATOMY

For the body is not one member but many.
1 Corinthians 12:14

✫ ✫ ✫

A little boy was asked to write an essay on the different parts of the human body (anatomy). Here is what he wrote:

"Your head is kind of round and hard, and your brains are in it and your hair, too. Your face is the front of your head where you eat and make faces. Your neck is what keeps your head out of your collar and it's hard to keep clean. Your shoulders are sort of shelves where you hook your suspenders on. Your stummick is something that if you don't eat often enough it hurts, and spinach don't help none. Your spine is a long bone in your back that keeps you from folding up. Your back is always behind you no matter how quick you turn around. Your arms you got to have to pitch with and so you can reach the butter. Your fingers stick out of your hands so you can throw a curve and add up rithmetick. Your legs is what if you have not got two of, you can't get to first base. Your feet are what you run on, your toes are what get stubbed. And that's all their is of you, except what's inside, and I never saw that."

Just as the human earth-suit has many parts with specific functions, so do we as a Christian family. The problem seems to be that we function more as individuals than as a family. We seem to have inserted the letter "I" in the word team. We all are different in the way we look, talk, act and function, but we have a common thread that is supposed to sew us together–Christ. Each one of us brings to the table a whole new set of goals and gifts used to further the kingdom as a body of believers. Think about it (I'll wait here!) . . . the hand has a separate function from the foot, the foot is different than the knee, the knee does not perform as an eye, and so on. As you look around, you'll notice that each Christian brings a different gift or talent to the family and together we mount a mighty force for the Kingdom. Now let's go team!

✫ ✫ ✫

Further Study: What do you feel your gifts are? Are you, at times, intimidated by others' gifts? Why? Do you function as a part or separate from the body?

WAYS TO HANDLE STRESS

A time to weep and a time to laugh.
Ecclesiastes 3:4

★ ★ ★

Wall need to grab a break from this treadmill of life from time to time. Since we are such creatures of habit, we need to break the mold, spread our wings, and just be strange for a minute . . . totally out of character. The following list is an example of some strange things we can do to handle those tough times in life. You can add to this list or take away, but hopefully, it will get your creative juices flowing down the funnel of fun. Take a look:

Pop some popcorn without putting the lid on.
Use your Mastercard to pay your Visa (just kidding).
When someone says, "Have a nice day," tell them you have other plans.
Forget the diet center and send yourself a candy gram.
Make a list of things to do that you've already done.
Dance in front of your pets.
Draw underwear on the natives in *National Geographic.*
Drive to work in reverse (a joke).
Reflect on your favorite episode of "The Flintstones" during class.
Refresh yourself: put your tongue on a frozen steel guardrail.
Start a funny rumor and see if you recognize it when it comes back.
Write a short story using alphabet soup.
Stare at people through a fork and pretend they are all in jail.
Make up a language and ask people for directions.
Put your clothes on backwards and pretend nothing's wrong (walk backward).

Note: these ideas are not to taken literally; they're just thought provokers. You make up your own list. Live a little!

★ ★ ★

Further Study: How often do you laugh? How do you handle stress? Do you take yourself too seriously at times? Why?

PEACE TREATY

He will stand and shepherd his flock in the strength of the Lord, in the majesty of the name of the Lord his God. And they will live securely, for then his greatness will reach to the ends of the earth. And He will be their peace.
Micah 5:4-5

★ ★ ★

Since George Washington's first inauguration in April of 1789 through Bill Clinton's reign, we have had wars and rumors of wars to live with. For the past 200 years of America's history, we have survived World War I and II, Korea, Vietnam, and most recently the Gulf War. The war that seems to have left its mark in our history books is the Civil War era. It was four years of vicious, devastating warfare that cost hundreds of thousands of lives, divided families and friends, and left half the country smoldering. The war was between the North's commercial economic structure (railroads, canals, steamships, etc.) and the South's agrarian slave-based economy, which provided cotton, tobacco, rice and corn. The simplest explanation for the war might be that the Southerners didn't want to be told how to live their lives. The struggle for control was a powder keg with a long burning fuse that ultimately exploded with horrifying results which we still see today.

As long as we all live on the same planet, there will be rumors of war. Where you have people, you have a difference in philosophies, ideas, and ways of doing things. Everyone always thinks his/her way is best and holds the mentality "my way or the highway." Take a look back since the division of Cain and Abel, and you'll see two paths, two ways. We all are looking for that plot of peace to seek shelter and refuge in, a quiet spot which is secure for ourselves and our families removed from the violence and destruction. Let me tell you that the only peace we'll ever have in this lifetime is with our Lord. He is the producer of peace, Savior of security and the refuge of redemption. He will stand between us and an angry world. He will fill the gap of peace and war, and finally, He will return to take us to that shelter in the sky we call heaven. He is the Prince of Peace, you know.

★ ★ ★

Further Study: If Webster's dictionary called you to define peace, what would you tell them? Where do you seek peace? Why do we want peace so badly?

HEY COACH . . . SPEARMINT

By this all men will know you are My disciples if you have love for one another.
John 13:35

★ ★ ★

One of the greatest movies to hit the screen in a long time was *Hoosiers*. Granted, I am an old basketball player, so it's no surprise it appealed to me. The story was set in a small farming town, in who-knows-where Indiana, which had a small school with a new coach (Gene Hackman). The suspense builds as the peon team begins to win and ultimately makes its way to the big time state championships in Indianapolis. During the final game they get thumped on by this big city team being led by a star post man. The head coach pulls his player aside and tells him to guard this big-time player so close that he will be able to tell the coach what flavor of gum he's chewing. A few minutes on the clock pass and the small town team starts their comeback. The player runs by the bench and yells, "Hey Coach . . . it's spearmint." The coach just grins and nods his head with pride.

We all need to take on that coaching strategy as we get to know other believers. We need to get so closely knit and united in spirit that we can tell someone what the other person's likes, dislikes, goals and dreams are. The only way to get to know someone in an intimate, deep-level capacity is through spending t-i-m-e. Friendships are no different than stocks, bonds and retirement funds. They are all an investment in your future. What "time" translates into is sacrifice, and sacrifice translates into dedication, and dedication into loyalty, and so on. You can clearly see that loving someone unconditionally is not a one-time thing . . . it's a process we all grow into with God and time. The young player's reward for getting so close to the other player was a championship . . . for you, companionship.

★ ★ ★

Further Study: What does loyalty mean to you? How could you really get close to a fellow believer today? Is it worth it to you? When are you gonna' start?

MALE MENTALITY

But these people are stubborn and have a rebellious heart.
Jeremiah 5:23

★ ★ ★

Between two farms near Valleyview, Alberta, you will find two fences running parallel for half a mile, only two feet apart. Why two fences when only one is necessary? Two farmers named Paul and Oscar had a disagreement that erupted into an all out feud. Paul wanted to build a fence between their land and split the cost, but Oscar disagreed and refused to contribute. Paul wanted to keep cattle on his land, so he went ahead and built the fence on his own. Afterward, Oscar said to Paul, "I see we have a fence now." "What do you mean we?" Paul replied. "I had the property line surveyed and built the fence two feet inside my property line, which means some of my land is outside the fence. Now if any of your cows step foot on my property, I'll shoot 'em for trespassing." Oscar knew this was not a joke, so when he eventually decided to use the land adjoining Paul's pasture, he was forced to build a second fence only two feet from the first. Oscar and Paul are both gone now, but their double fence stands as a monument to the high price paid for stubbornness.

It's amazing just what sparks a "tiff" between people. Often folks are all out to win with no regard for the feelings or concerns of others. It's the "my way or the highway" mentality that gets most of us in trouble. Why can't we have a servant's attitude and heart when it comes to dealing with each other? Don't you realize we were all placed on the same planet for a reason? "Getting along" is only difficult when we create an environment (with attitude and behavior) that makes it difficult. What if Christ had an attitude that only exalted Me, Myself and I? (Answer: We'd be in a pickle about now!) Learn to live in harmony, not harassment. Give a little, and you'll get a lot.

★ ★ ★

Further Study: Are you a stubborn person? What makes you want to be stubborn (specific areas)? Does having a "my way" attitude make life easier or more difficult? How can you work on that area?

THE BOA CONSTRICTOR

*Now the serpent was more crafty than any beast of the
field which the Lord God had made.*
Genesis 3:1

★ ★ ★

I have a big problem with reptiles that slither on their bellies and
scare the pants off people. In college my bright roommate decided life was-
n't exciting enough, so he purchased a rather large boa constrictor snake.
That's right . . . a third roomie–one that eats people and never sleeps. My
roommate (not the slimy one) fed his new found companion (named Bert)
rats for an afternoon snack. Yuck-eee! You talk about gross! Can you
believe you can actually purchase rats to use for snake food? Don't rats
have a humane society to protect them? (Guess not . . . who has a rat for
a pet anyway? Don't answer that!) Let me get to my point. I always
thought that constrictors squeezed their prey to death, then ate it whole.
Not true–these snakes wrap their slithery bodies around a victim, wait for
them to exhale and squeeze down. Wait for an exhale, squeeze down,
another exhale, squeeze tighter until the prey can't inhale again and finally dies.

Do you recall anyone in the Bible who could possibly go by the code
name "Serpent?" I believe he first made his debut on stage in the Broadway
hit, "In The Garden." Satan is (notice I didn't say was) a constrictor of life
who squeezes the joy out of life when we fall prey to sin. Whether pre-
marital sex, compulsive dishonesty, bitterness, or hatred, sin will choke you
out like a candle with no oxygen. Steer clear of the serpent and his deceiving tactics of tightening that will result in death (physical and spiritual).
Believe you me, having a snake as a roommate was bad, but as a master, it
would be worse.

★ ★ ★

Further Study: Why was Satan called a serpent? What does it mean in the
verse above that the snake was more crafty than any beast of the field?
What does Satan tighten down on in your life to squeeze the joy out of
being a Christian?

GET READY

Be ye therefore ready also.
Luke 12:40

✦ ✦ ✦

One of the greatest needs today is to be a Christian ready to face Christ at any turn. This is about as easy as eating soup with a fork. The biggest battle in our journey is not against sin, difficulties or circumstances, but against being so wrapped up in what we do in our daily trek that we aren't ready to face Christ around the next corner. Our one great need is not for a defining creed or figuring out if we are of any value to God, but to be ready to face Him. The funny (mostly scary) thing about this subject is that Jesus rarely comes when or where we expect. Rather, we find Him when we least expect and always in the most illogical situations and circumstances. The only way a believer can keep true to our Lord is by being ready for His surprise visits. It's not what we are doing, but who we are in the deep closets of our soul that is important. He wants our lives to reflect the attitude of child-wonder. If we honestly want to "be ready" for Jesus, we must stop being religious and be spiritually sincere. Our culture will stereotype you as impractical and dreamy if you live out a life of "looking off to Jesus," but when He does appear in the midst of a trial, or when the heat is turned up in your life, you will be the only one who is ready. Don't trust, obey, follow or listen to anyone, even the finest saint who ever walked this planet, if they hinder your sight of Christ. Get ready today, don't wait for tomorrow . . . it could be too late.

✦ ✦ ✦

Further Study: If Christ were to come today, this very minute, would you be ready? What do you need to do to get yourself ready? What does "ready" mean? Describe who you know that you feel is ready.

SEEKING YOUR SAVIOR

There is no Savior besides me.
Isaiah 43:11

★ ★ ★

The sun had just risen over the small village of Plelo in German-occupied France on a hot summer day in 1944. A 15-year-old boy didn't understand why he and his community had been brought before a firing squad in the town square. Maybe it was because they had hidden out from a unit of Marquisards (French underground freedom fighters), or perhaps merely to satisfy the blood-thirsty German commander's need for revenge. No matter the reason, they knew they were about to die. As the young boy stood in front of the firing squad, memories of childhood began to pop into his mind—running around the French countryside, playing in the streets, kick-ball games. Most of all, he feared the feeling of bullets entering his body. He hoped no one would see his tears or hear his cries, so he exhaled and closed his eyes. Suddenly, he heard exploding mortar behind the building, tanks rolling into town. The German firing squad ran for cover and the boy saw a unit of U.S. tanks led by Bob Hamsley. After three hours, 50 Nazis were dead and another 50 were taken prisoner. In 1990 the town of Plelo honored Captain Hamsley on the very spot (town square) where dozens of village residents were nearly executed. The man who initiated the search for Hamsley and the ceremony honoring him was the former 15-year-old boy. He was determined to find the man who saved his life and honor him.

This is a touching story about remembering and honoring a savior. What a neat testimony of a man who was indebted to a savior (Captain Hamsley) and refused to go through life without recognizing him. Never forget the Savior (Jesus) who rescued you.

★ ★ ★

Further Study: Do you forget your Savior? Why? How can you honor Him? Will you? How? When?

I Give You My Word

Let your yes be yes and your no be no.
James 5:12

★ ★ ★

The Boy Scout Oath: "On my honor I will do my best to do my duty to God and my country and to obey the Scout Law; to help other people at all times; to keep myself physically strong, mentally awake and morally straight."

There it is, just as easy to quote now as it was when I was younger. This oath is what every Boy and Girl Scout promises to live. This life in which we live is full of oaths. You see it when the President of the United States takes office, you repeat it before you take the witness stand in a court of law, you'll be in awe of it when two people are exchanging rings at the altar for marriage, and you read it when Moses came down from Mt. Sinai glowing after his encounter with God Almighty. I realize that saying and living are on two sides of the freeway. It's one thing to put your hand up or mumble the words, but following through and committing to what you just said is tough.

We seem to have lost something other than our wallet or car keys from prior generations. I'm not sure if they forgot to teach us, we didn't listen or maybe we just don't see the value in it. What? Your word. It's a rare quality to see surviving today when someone gives you his word and also follows through with the commitment. When someone says he will be there at 2:00 and he arrives 10 minutes early, you can bet on it. In a society of red tape and paper work, we could sure do ourselves a favor by closing out business contracts with a handshake and a verbal commitment instead of a novel of words. How about teachers giving you a test and letting you take it home on your word that you won't cheat, or committing to your date's parents that you will go where you promise to go? Promises and oaths are interchangeable words, and whether you're a Scout or a Christian, they are worth taking and keeping for the rest of your life.

★ ★ ★

Further Study: How good is your word? Why is it so tough to commit to a promise? Is your word good today?

A Coach's Perspective

That they (people of Israel) *may see and recognize, and consider and gain insight as well, that the hand of the Lord has done this.*
Isaiah 41:10

★ ★ ★

It was the summer of 1970, and I was playing for the Dallas Little League All-Star team under Coach Hayden Fry, now coach of the University of Iowa football team. Coach had a rule that no one could steal a base unless he first gave the sign. This upset me a lot because I felt I knew the pitchers and catchers well enough to tell when I could and couldn't steal. In one game I decided to steal without a sign from Coach (mistake). I got a good jump off the pitcher and easily beat the throw to second base. After I shook the dirt off my uniform, I smiled with delight, feeling proud of myself. After the game, Coach Fry took me aside and explained why he hadn't given me the sign to steal and why what I did was foolish. The batter behind me was Eddie, the homerun slugger. When I stole second, first base was left open, so the other team walked the slugger intentionally, taking the bat out of his hands. The next batter hadn't been hitting the ball well, so Coach intended to send in a pinch hitter to try and drive in the men (me) on base. That left Coach Fry without bench strength later in the game when he needed it.

The problem was, I saw only my capability to steal. Coach Fry was watching the whole game, not just one inning. We too, see only so far, but God sees the bigger picture. When He sends us a signal, it's wise to obey, no matter how much we may think we know. God is the coach in the game of life because we aren't capable. Listen and obey, it's the only way.

★ ★ ★

Further Study: Have you ever done anything on your own call despite warnings from your authority? Did you blow the game for your team, family, friends?

How Do You Know?

But the prophet who shall speak a word presumptuously in My name which I have not commanded him to speak in the name of other gods, that prophet shall die.

Deuteronomy 18:20

★ ★ ★

What comes to your mind when you hear the word "prophet?" Do you think of someone of high intelligence, royal or divine insight; someone who is over qualified and underpaid? If you were to die today, go to heaven and find yourself sitting down at a table next to or across from Habakkuk, Amos, Zephaniah, Haggai, Malachi, Obadiah, Zechariah, Hosea, Joel or Ezra, would you ask them . . . "Now who are you guys?" The other two-thirds of your Bible is filled with former or latter prophets who were appointed by Yahweh to be spokespersons for Him. They may have come under the title of seer, servant, messenger, man of God or sons of prophets. The proof that they were legitimate was if they spoke in the name of God, spoke by revelation or inspiration, had high moral character, had a true call of God, if their message was authenticated by signs, if their message was in agreement with previous revelation and if there was fulfillment of predictions. Their goal was to edify and encourage the believers in God into a deeper, more obedient relationship with Him.

It is important to distinguish between popular conceptions of who were prophets and those who were truly chosen by God. Jesus demonstrated prophetic characteristics in His message, predictions of the future, being sent by God, speaking only words of the Father, and in His ministry. 1 Corinthians 13:8 says that prophecy will cease, but it doesn't say when. A false prophet was not the same as a pagan prophet because false prophets were and are prophesying in the name of God (Yahweh). My purpose here is not to figure out if there are or are not modern day prophets. It's to get you excited about the prophets in your Bible so you will study them and to educate you on who they are. I want you to have a foundation of knowledge to call their "bluff" when someone you see or hear claims to be a prophet, yet his/her qualifications don't match up to those in Deuteronomy 18. Beware!

★ ★ ★

Further Study: Read the qualifications to be a prophet of Yahweh in Deuteronomy 18:15-22. How can you tell in our culture today if someone is a "true" or "false" prophet? What are you to do if you find yourself being led by a false prophet?

HALF FULL OR HALF EMPTY

Caleb quieted the people before Moses and said, "We should by all means go up and take possession of it; we shall overcome it." But the other men had gone up with him too and said, "We are not able to go up against the people for they are too strong for us."
Numbers 13:30-31

✯ ✯ ✯

A great test to see if people are optimists or pessimists is to show them a clear glass containing water up to the half-way point. Now ask if the glass is half empty or half full. You will find most of the time that the majority will view the glass of water as half empty. This is not wrong, just a fact. Most people always see situations in life as half empty, too. The masses will, most of the time, see life's negatives far before they see its positives.

If you have ever read the story of Joshua and Caleb, you have read a story of two perspectives. In a nutshell God has told the people of Israel that the "Land of Milk and Honey" is theirs for the taking. A bunch of spies (or scouts) are sent into the land of Canaan to check it out and bring back a report of its condition. They were to find out if the land was safe, had good pastures, grew good vegetation and would be a good home for three million new Israelite residents. Of all the scouts only two came back positive; the rest saw a glass half empty. Yes, the land was perfect, but it did have a few bugs to work out, namely, mean thugs called Amelikites who could be dealt with. God calls you daily to go into your home, school, clubs, team, or circle of friends and take a stand, take up residency for Him. Yes, it will be tough, and there will be opposition, but remember He took care of them on the cross at Calvary. Will you return to Him as the majority with a half empty report or a Joshua and Caleb report of half full? Think about it.

✯ ✯ ✯

Further Study: How do you view the cup? Do you see more negative in God's plans or positive? Do you feel you are an overcomer and capable of accomplishing anything with Him? Why or why not?

ASSOCIATE STAFF

For all that is in the world, the lust of the flesh and the lust of the eyes and the boastful pride of life, is not from the Father, but is from the world.
1 John 2:16

* * *

The more you look like Christ, the more the world is gonna' treat you like Him. It is a frightening thing when you arrive at the point in your spiritual journey that you decide to truly be an ambassador for Jesus. The scary part about it is that when you pledge allegiance to the flag of America, you live and associate as a citizen of America. However, when you pledge allegiance to Christ, you disassociate yourself from the world and proclaim heaven as your homeland. Being a Christian is more than walking down the aisle, attending church or wearing a cross. The price Jesus paid was a heavy one. You may not get ridiculed and alienated when you associate with a church, youth group, Bible study or religious movement, but you do when you say, "I'm a follower of Jesus Christ." The penalty (really a privilege) is when you finally come to that point of locking arms with Christ.

Years ago a country song summed up what being a real Christian in a real hurting world is all about . . . "If you don't stand for something, then you'll fall for anything." The "something" has got to be Jesus. The "anything" might be sex, money, status, cults, and so on. Ask God to plant deep in the chambers of your heart a soul of passion to follow Him, knowing that the cost will include pain and suffering. I don't know where folks get off on all this hoopla that Christianity is a total joy ride. Either I am reading a different Bible, or they are not hearing the truth that the adventure, called Christianity, takes endurance and perseverance. Pain is a part of the curriculum of God's classroom, so prepare for a tough test, but one worth passing.

* * *

Further Study: Why is association with Christ so costly? To whom do people say you are pledged? How can you handcuff yourself to Christ from now on? Why is ridicule a part of Christianity?

A FASHION STATEMENT

Likewise I want women to adorn (dress) *themselves with
proper clothing, modestly and discreetly.*
1 Timothy 2:9

★ ★ ★

Look no further than your local newsstand to see the latest styles
trickling down the fashion pipe of the world. *Vogue, Seventeen, GQ,
Glamour, Self, Fashion & Design, Elle,* and of course, *Cosmopolitan* to name a
few. Fashion in this world of ours changes as often as weather patterns.
One minute you're making a fashion "statement," and the next you're
frowned upon as being out-of-date. If I have this figured out, the way I see
it is that if you just hang on to the same clothes for a few years, they'll
come back in style (i.e. bell bottoms, neons, wide ties, etc.). Now don't get
me wrong, some things will never be out-to-lunch, but that's not the norm.
Psychologists claim that there are several ways people show their inward
desires in an outward expression. For example, what we desire can be seen
in the sort of car we drive, hairstyle we sport and clothes we wear. The
only problem with this "expression" is that it seems to be moving in the
"less is better" direction. The shorter the dress or shorts, the tighter the
pants, the more high cut and revealing the swim-suit the better . . . for
who?

I know about right now you have decided this whole devotion is targeted at the female and yep, that's a good guess. Why? Because women are
like a crock pot (heat up slowly), and men are like a microwave (heat up
fast). In other words, men are turned on by sight much easier than women.
So when they see a "cute young thing" running around half clothed, they
get aroused quickly, which in turn leads to lustful thoughts (Philippians
4:8). Please, I beg of you, from the knees of all men trying to seek God's
ways on everything, watch what you wear and how you present yourself
to men. I don't know of anything that can steal a man's heavenly perspective quicker than a worldly outfit. I'm not telling you to buy all your clothes
at the local Thrift Store, but I am asking you to ask yourself one question
before you step into your closet or throw down the credit card . . . how
comfortable would you feel if Jesus stepped into the room while you were
wearing what you had on? Make a fashion statement for Jesus . . . dress
modestly.

★ ★ ★

Further Study: Do you dress modestly or risky? How does this affect the
opposite sex? What does Luke 17:2 mean?

GROWTH CHART

I planted, Apollos watered, but God causes the growth.
1 Corinthians 3:6

★ ★ ★

Growing up can be one of the most fun experiences in life. Three sons fill our house with wrestling, war, GI Joe's, monster grocery lists, scabby knees, dirty clothes and intense competition—you can imagine the total chaos. We measure the boys each month on a growth chart attached to the wall. One day, the chart slipped from the wall, and my oldest son, Daniel, tried to re-hang it. As he did, the chart slipped off the nail and rested flush with the floor . . . about four inches short of the real height. Daniel got his brother, Dustin, up against the chart the next day, then came running into the room yelling, "Mommy! Mommy! Dustin grew four inches this month." My wife responded, "That's impossible, he's only two years old. Let's go see." They walked up to the bedroom where suspicions were confirmed—the chart was set at an improper height.

We can easily repeat Daniel's mistake in gauging our spiritual growth. Compared to a shortened scale, we may appear better than we are, or more mature in Christ. It is only when we stand against the cross, that "great leveler of men" (as A.T. Robertson called it), that we cannot think of ourselves more highly than we should. Jesus must be the standard against which we measure ourselves. When we stand against friends or society, we elevate our spiritual mentality. Match up with Christ, and you'll remain focused and on track. Growth is a slow, steady, daily process that takes time and effort through Christ to accomplish.

★ ★ ★

Further Study: Do you compare yourself to others? To what standard do you compare yourself? How do you match up? What is the danger of comparing yourself to worldly standards?

A CHAIN REACTION

Pilate had a notice prepared and fastened to the cross. It read:
"Jesus of Nazareth, King of the Jews."
John 19:19

★ ★ ★

It took place in Los Alamos on May 21, 1946, and it involved a young scientist performing an experiment necessary for testing the atomic bomb in the waters of the south Pacific at Bikini. He'd successfully completed the experiment several times before, but this test would be different. In an effort to determine the amount of U-235 needed for a chain reaction, he would push two hemispheres of uranium together. Then, just at critical mass, he would push them apart with his screwdriver (sounds real hi-tech to me), instantly stopping the chain reaction. As he was about to separate the masses, the screwdriver slipped and the hemispheres of uranium came too close together. Instantly, the room was filled with a bluish haze. Young Louis Slotin reacted and instead of diving for cover and maybe saving himself, he tore the two hemispheres apart bare-handed, thus stopping the chain reaction. By this heroic act, he saved the lives of seven others in the lab, but exposed himself to the dangerous radiation of Uranium 235. Nine days later, he died in agony, but his colleagues survived.

Nineteen centuries ago the Son of the living God walked directly into sin's most concentrated radiation and willingly allowed Himself to be touched by its curse (death). But get this, by this heroic act of courage on the cross, He broke the chain reaction of a sinful world with no hope for a future and broke the power of sin that began in the laboratory of Eden. He died so that you and I might walk away unharmed into the glory of heaven—what a deal!

★ ★ ★

Further Study: What do you feel is the most significant event in the Bible? Why? Is what Christ did on the cross important in your life? Do you see Jesus as a modern-day hero, or a forgotten fable?

WIZARD OF OZ

And the God of peace will soon crush Satan under your feet,
and the grace of our Lord Jesus will be with you.
Romans 16:20

★ ★ ★

They seem to be household names in all generations. Dorothy, Toto, Scarecrow, Tin Man, Cowardly Lion and the Wicked Witch are the familiar characters in *The Wizard of Oz*, along with scenes of flying monkeys, dark and mysterious castles, a city of emerald green, bright red slippers, the yellow brick road and a farmhouse spinning up to heaven. My personal favorite adventure in Oz is the way Dorothy got back to Kansas. The intimidating Wizard first required items scavenged from the Wicked Witch. The gang returned with the items, but the big Oz reneged on the deal and tried to run them off. It looked as if there'd be no brain for the Scarecrow, no courage for the Lion, no heart for the Tin Man, and definitely no plane ticket for Dorothy and Toto . . . that is, until the little rat-dog went around back and pulled back the curtain to expose a harmless, little, gray-haired man, claiming to be the Wizard of Oz.

Satan, the fierce lion that roams the earth stalking his victims, is in reality a pussycat. Yes, he does have a lot of tricks up his sleeve, but he was defeated once and for all on a hill called Calvary. The crucifixion of Jesus proved Satan's lack of power and exposed him for what he is . . . a wimp of a wizard. As a Christian, you are capable of disarming this enemy and his ragged brigade of blundering bean-headed demons at any given moment. You have no need to fear the enemy, but you must be wise to his deceiving smoke-screens. No matter your age, size or years you have been a believer (Toto was a small dog, notice), you can defeat this enemy with a wave of your Christ-like wand. Click your heels together and say, "I am a winner" three times. You will eventually go home, not to Kansas, but heaven.

★ ★ ★

Further Study: Are you aware of Satan? Are you scared of him? Think about all the power of Christ you have in your life to defeat and expose him.

PRUNING

Those whom I love, I rebuke and disciple; be excited and therefore repent.
Revelation 3:19

★ ★ ★

Growing up in an area with lots of trees, many of which planted themselves right smack in the middle of my frontyard, was fun but exhausting. As you know, where trees abound, so does a multitude of leaves each fall. People visiting our home used to make this awful big deal about the beautiful fall foliage, but it foreshadowed raking and bagging to me. Every year, like a tradition, my father and I would recover out of storage the chainsaw and go to pruning the monster pecan trees, all 21 of them. Talk about a task that seemed endless! It was almost like we were creating more of a mess than making an improvement. Consider the viewpoint of the tree also. Man, did I think that all that cutting and cracking would produce some awful pain (if trees do feel). My dad could make a 30 foot high massive tree look like a nub in just a matter of a few coarse cuts. Little did my feeble mind know that this whole process was for the benefit, not the harm, of the trees' future growth. God, too, periodically goes and gets His spiritual saw and begins to trim off areas in your life that don't look like or act like His Son Jesus. Once as I watched a woodcarver chisel on a block of wood, another observer asked him what he was making. "An Indian warrior," the woodcarver replied. "How do you know which parts to carve away?" the onlooker then asked. "Everything that doesn't look like an Indian," said the carver.

God's purpose in discipling you is to make you better, not to kill or destroy you. Realize He only does this pruning because He loves you. Your parents only put parameters and rules around you because they care, not because they want to hurt you. God only wants you to succeed in this journey we call Christianity, and one way is to prune off the dead or heavy branches which could eventually destroy the tree (you). Next time your God or your loving parents prune away on you, look past the momentary pain and see the benefits that will come . . . a person who looks more like Jesus.

★ ★ ★

Further Study: How has God pruned you lately? Did you feel His love? How do your parents show they care?

BACK TO THE BASICS

*In those days there was no king of Israel; everyone
did what was right in their own eyes.*
Judges 21:25

★ ★ ★

Americans have been slow to see that as the old moral map fades, we won't be left with another alternative, but with no map at all. "Sin" by the end of the 19th century was fading as a belief, and how could it be otherwise. After all, sin means transgression against God. In our culture God has been replaced by fortune, and fortune makes no moral judgments. Evil has turned into bad luck, and good luck became the new benediction. To pray for the grace of God has become more embarrassing than to hope for luck. This way of thinking has changed the meaning of death, since there is no one to whom the dying are going. People are so busy "doing" that they forget why they are doing; we have become occupied with routine pleasures that are fading fast. We are a people who are going, but are not sure where. We are a culture with no rules, guidelines, morals, values, virtues, standards, law and no god.

We as a body of believers need to get back to the basics. Vince Lombardi, the diciest coach of the Super Bowl champs, was famous for coming into the locker room after a Green Bay Packer loss, tossing a football in his hand and explaining to his pro athletes that "this is a football." In other words, we are gonna' have to get back to the basics if we are to win for Christ in our culture.

#1 Sola Scriptura : scripture alone
#2 Solus Christus : Faith alone
#3 Sola Gratia : Grace alone
#4 Sola Fide : To Him be all the Glory!

If we as believers will get back to the foundations of our faith in God and live out these four points, people will be in awe of our Savior. People in our society see so much hypocrisy, deceit, failure and wishy-washy standards it's no wonder they aren't impressed by us or our God. God's Word and our faith, grace lived out in T-shirts and tennis shoes in our earth suits, will bring glory to our Lord and Savior. This sort of lifestyle will bring repentance and national reformation, which is much needed at this stage of the game . . . don't ya' think?

★ ★ ★

Further Study: Why do we as a whole make our faith so complicated?

SEARCH AND RESCUE

For the Son of Man has come to seek and to save that which was lost.
Luke 19:10

★ ★ ★

On the night of April 15, 1912, the Titanic sunk to the floor of the Atlantic, some two and a half hours after hitting an iceberg that tore a 300 foot gash in her starboard side. Although 20 life-boats and rafts were launched, they were too few and only partially filled. Most passengers ended up struggling in the icy seas while those in the life boats waited a safe distance from the sinking vessel. Lifeboat #14 did row back after the "unsinkable" ship slipped from sight to chase cries in the darkness, seeking to save a precious few. No other boat joined #14 for the rescue mission (even though they were only about half full), fearing that a swarm of unknown swimmers might flip their safe boat and swamp them in the frigid seas. Members of the rescue mission that eventually found the life-boats never quite understood how fear (selfish fear) could prompt the survivors to not help as they watched hundreds die in the violent sea that night.

In His mission statement, Jesus says that He has "come to seek and save" and has commissioned us to do the same. I find that most Christians have good hearts and a willing spirit, but they often go down in defeat to the arch rival, fear. While people drown in the treacherous waters around us, we are tempted to stay all safe and dry and make certain no one rocks our security boat. What we don't understand is that the life boats aren't our own, so safety comes only at the expense of the One who overcame His fear with love to save us. Don't let the security and safety of your present position as an heir to the Kingdom, and the fear of rejection, stop you from throwing a life-line to the lost souls bobbing around your daily life. Paddle, boy . . . paddle!

★ ★ ★

Further Study: Do you fear sharing Jesus with someone else? Are you sitting in your nice, safe, cozy world watching and hearing the cries of the drowning victims? Make it your goal to tell a lost person about the love of Jesus today? (Fear later!)

CHRIST IN THE CRISIS

Show yourself an example of those who believe.
1 Timothy 4:12

★ ★ ★

There's an interesting account of a lady named Judy Anderson, who grew up as the daughter of a missionary in Zaire. As a little girl, she went to a day-long rally celebrating the 100th anniversary of Christian missionaries coming to Zaire. After a long day of speeches and festive music, an old man came out of the crowd and insisted that he be allowed to speak. He told the crowd that he soon would die and that he alone had some important information to share. He explained that when the missionaries came 100 years before, his people thought they were strange and their message unusual. The tribal leaders decided to test the missionaries by slowly poisoning them to death. Over a period of months and years, all the missionaries and their families died one by one. The old man said, "It was as we watched how they died that we decided we wanted to live as Christians."

That story had gone untold for 100 years. Those faithful followers died and never knew why they were dying. They stayed true to their tasks and loyal to their Lord, not knowing what an impact, even to their last few breaths, they made on thousands of viewers who saw Christ in the crisis. You don't have to be in Africa or a missionary for folks to see the Christ in you. It's easy to be a Christian during those high times, but what about when you're in the valleys of life? Are you gonna' be one of those followers who takes Christ with you, even to your grave? I hope and pray so!

★ ★ ★

Further Study: Do people see Christ in the middle of your crisis? How much impact does your every reaction have on others? How many eyes watch you even though you're not aware of them?

SHINE JESUS SHINE

The lamp of the body is the eye, if therefore your eye is clear,
your whole body will be full of light.
Matthew 6:22

★ ★ ★

Talk about an outdoor experience! Little did I know when I accepted an invitation to go on an elk hunting trip in a five-million acre wilderness in Idaho, it would be such an adventure! Our trusty guide led us for five days over 9,000-foot mountain tops and through pine forests in search of the "Big One." The lessons about life in general and the parallels of my Christian life were as plentiful as mountain daisies in the springtime.

Our home was a tent, our water from a spring, our food . . . home cooked, and our transportation . . . horses and mules (look out wagon train!). Little did I know I would only get four to five hours of sleep a night and be on the back of a horse five hours a day. Each morning at 4:00 a.m. we would ride out of camp straight up the mountains in pitch dark on a 12 inch wide trail next to thousand foot cliffs where only the horse could see, searching for the bugle of a bull elk, relying solely on the eyes of our horse and guide. Never before have I depended on one of the five senses so heavily for my safety and my success in a hunt.

In one of the greatest sermons ever accounted, Jesus refers to the eye in a unique manner. Matthew 6:22 tells us that the "lamp of the body is the eye." The verse goes on to say "if your eye is clear, your whole body will be full of light." What worldly items clog our vision of God? What can you do at home to keep your eye clear? What does the lost society in which we live see if we shine for Christ? During a ride on my horse "Jock," I realized how much we rely on our eyes (the hot-line to our hearts) to guide us toward our goal . . . not elk, but living for Christ. I understood how TV, movies, books and magazines can cause us to be spiritually blind, making us vulnerable as prey. Take a minute to look in a mirror at those beautiful eyes and see if the lamp is lit. If it's dim in there, do what it takes to get it shining brightly again.

★ ★ ★

Further Study: Have you had an eye exam from the Savior lately? How's your light burning today?

Drink for Thought

Be not drunk with wine but, be filled with the Spirit.
Ephesians 5:18

☆ ☆ ☆

It can spell T-R-O-U-B-L-E for all of us, and it is the most dangerous drug in general use in our culture today. Pay close attention to this. I am by no means insinuating or tying to "make" you believe one way or another, yet I feel convicted to share this knowledge with you. The Bible gives 637 references to drink or drinking. In those references there are a number of different words which are translated "wine." To fully understand ancient Jewish culture, versus our contemporary western culture, we need to take a look at some of these words.

In the Old Testament there are three key Hebrew words: 1) "yayin," 2) "shekar" and 3) "tirosh." The first word occurs 140 times and is a general term for all classes of wine, alcoholic, and non-alcoholic fermented or unfermented grape beverages. These are mixed or diluted with water. The second word occurs 23 times and is in reference to "strong drink" or unmixed with water. The third word is used 38 times and is often called "sweet wine" or "grape juice." In the New Testament you find 3 Greek terms: 1) "oinos," 2) "sikera" and 3) "gleukos." "Oinos," counterpart to the Old Testament "yayin," is used 33 times; in the process of fermentation it was diluted with water. "Sikera," whose counterpart in the Old Testament was "shekar," means strong drink or unmixed wine. "Gleukos," whose counterpart is "tirosh," refers to "new wine."

O.K. . . . now, what does all this have to do with anything? Distillation was not discovered until about 1500 AD. You can't get around the fact that scripture condemns drunkenness, yet the question arises: "Are today's beer and wine alcohol levels considered to be strong drink?" Biblical "wine" was 2.5% to 2.75% after a 3 to 1 water to wine mixture. "Strong drink" in Biblical times was from 3% to 11% and those who consumed it are described in scripture as "barbarian." All of this is to say that it's your responsibility and personal spirit-felt convictions (via scripture) that need to guide you, not a devotion. Obviously being under age and consuming alcohol is illegal and wrong, along with getting drunk. After that, you make the call. I am not trying to be your holy spirit or sway you, just get you thinking and studying.

☆ ☆ ☆

Further Study: Read: Proverbs 23:20, Romans 13:13, Galatians 5:19 & 21, 1 Corinthians 6:9-11, Proverbs 20:21 and 23:29-31, John 2:10, Luke 1:15, Proverbs 31:6 and Proverbs 3: 9-10.

LET THE GAMES BEGIN

I give you this charge: Preach the word; be prepared in season and out of season; correct, rebuke and encourage with great patience and careful instruction.
2 Timothy 4:2

★ ★ ★

When September rolls around and there is a cool, crisp, nip in the air, the smell of football season is a reality. Friday night football heroes begin to shine under the stadium lights like stars on a dark night. Where I grew up in Texas, the only thing that was worse than missing Sunday church was failing to make it to the hometown high school football game (and that was serious).

We seem to live our lives from season to season, waiting for the next sporting event to transpire. As an athlete competing in these events, you know the time, sacrifice and dedication it takes to pull off a victory on Friday night. Spectators only see a small percentage of what it takes to compete at a winning level and miss the months and hours of prior-to-season preparation training. Paul (the head coach) teaches his player (Timothy) a few lessons and game plans which he, through his years of experience as a competitor, learned about being a Christian player. The book of 2 Timothy is the last book that the apostle Paul wrote before his death. Can you imagine, as his pupil, how you would hang on every last word of wisdom? One of the last gold nuggets of truth given to Timothy was to train, not only in season, but also during the off-season. Championships are won, not during season, but in the off-season training in the weight rooms, on the track and in the gyms after hours. Anyone can be motivated when there are people in the grandstands. Anyone can draw strength from within when the crowd roars with encouragement. But what about when there are no stands and no noise? We, as Christians, always need to be in spiritual training. We continually need to be using God's game plan (His word) to encourage and lead our friends down the narrow path of a championship life walking close to the Savior. If you think that a good cross-town rivalry game is exciting, try God's game . . . it's the best game goin'.

★ ★ ★

Further Study: What ways can you train today for God's game in the upcoming season?

COACH BUMBLEBEE

You became obedient from the heart to that form
of teaching to which you were committed.
Romans 6:17

★ ★ ★

He was like no man I'd ever seen or been around in all my years. If you looked up the word self-discipline in the dictionary, you'd find his picture next to it. He was a boxing coach for a youth club out of Seattle, Washington, and was training two teenage boxers for a national match that could lead to the 1996 Olympics. The tournament was scheduled to take place in Colorado Springs at the Olympic Training Facility where 350 young boxers were trying to be the next Foreman, Frazier or Ali. This coach went by the name "Coach Bumble-Bee," because aeronautically, bumble-bees shouldn't be able to fly, since their wings are too small for the size of their bodies. But the bees don't know that, so they fly anyway.

Coach Bumble-Bee, now 50 years old, was the driver in a serious bus accident that left him paralyzed from the waist down. For five and a half years he managed his life from a wheelchair until one day, after years of prayer and exercise, Coach began moving his legs again. Today, Coach Bumble-Bee is walking, running, lifting weights and jumping rope with his team members as he works out daily with them in vigorous training.

What faith! What determination! What discipline! What a deal! Told he would never walk again by physicians, but today not only walking, but running. I learned just through watching him work out with his boxers what it means to "never give up on God." The key ingredient to faith is commitment. Trust in God that He is bigger than theories, doctors' analysis and scientific data. You can be a bumble-bee too if you will turn a deaf ear to the crowd of doubters and focus on the Savior. God is and always will be bigger than any problem or situation you get yourself into. If you don't believe me . . . just go watch the bumble-bee fly.

★ ★ ★

Further Study: What does it mean to you to never give up? What makes you want to give up in tough times? What could you do to deepen that never-say-die attitude? Who could help you? Call 'em.

FENCE WALKERS

Where will you be stricken again, as you continue in your rebellion?
The whole head is sick and the whole heart is faint.
Isaiah 1:5

★ ★ ★

Growing up on a ranch all my life sure didn't make me a cowboy or farmer by any stretch of the imagination. One thing it did do is educate me in a few areas that I most likely would have slept through if it were taught in a classroom. One of my father's adventures was in the cattle ranching industry for a "short" while. I learned a few interesting tidbits about the nature of a cow. First of all, while buying cows at an auction barn (a real adventure), you can't tell which ones will turn out to be producers and which ones may be a problem. The first test comes when you first turn out the new cows into the pasture they'll soon call "home on the range." One of two things will happen. They'll either adapt to the new living arrangements, or they'll begin to walk the fence line to find a hole and escape captivity. I recall my dad just waiting there the first few hours to see which ones would run through the fence. He would immediately trailer those cows back up and take them to the slaughter house for processing into hamburgers and steaks. Once a fence walker, always a fence walker, and they're not worth the trouble of keeping.

Some folks are no different than a cow in that they always look for ways of breaking the barriers (fences) of life, Christian or not. Some folks walk the fences instead of roaming freely in the pasture God has given them. They look for loopholes in scripture, school, sports, business, family, and commitment. We as Christians can be different. We can live freely and enjoy all that we do have, instead of focusing on the few areas of no-no's we have been warned to stay clear of by God and His Word. Rebellious attitudes and behaviors do nothing but get us in trouble which eventually lead to destruction of our own lives. Don't be a fence walker, but be a pasture dweller for God. It's that one loophole that will eventually strangle us and send us to the packing plant.

★ ★ ★

Further Study: What areas of your walk with Christ do you try to escape? Why do you do it? What perspective can we have that will allow us to see all the positives of fences (rules) and not focus on the few negatives?

SIFTED

Simon, Simon, behold, Satan has demanded permission to sift you like wheat.
Luke 22:31

★ ★ ★

Take a moment to read in your Bible the verses prior to this one, beginning at verse 24. Do you see it? Do you see a gold nugget of scripture? What rich verses, full of knowledge and wisdom! We are all trying to make it to the top. We are all striving after a goal or reward that we think (false security) might fill the void in the pit of our stomachs. The problem is that to go up we must first go down, to win we must lose, to gain we must die . . . be sifted. The word sifted means to be separated, strained, screened and sorted out (doesn't sound like fun). If you think about it for a minute, there are only three things we bring to the table–time, talent, and treasure. That's it. No more, no less. Today we are either building upon our kingdom or God's kingdom. When we build on ourselves, we show the world statues in our memory, trophies accepted on our behalf. What is amazing about these treasures of self is that we aren't going to take them with us in eternity. God treasures those who are selfless, those who leave behind a Godly heritage, not an inheritance. Here is a little insight . . . you will not build a treasure for God until you have been "sifted" like wheat. Why? Because the process of sifting out self includes pain and suffering. Sifting is good for our maturing process and can only be accomplished by a divine God who knows what needs to be sifted out of our spiritual lives. Dying to self is a long, hard, process, but worth it when it comes to harvesting a good product.

★ ★ ★

Further Study: What are your talents? How are you using them today? Who gets the credit? Have you ever been sifted before? Was it a good or bad experience? Why or why not? What selfish desires do you think God needs to sift out of your life before He will use you?

DREAM TEAM

Where there is no vision, people perish.
Proverbs 29:18

★ ★ ★

You're never too old for a trip to see Mickey and Minnie Mouse. No place on this planet, I believe, has more fun rides, atmosphere or a better theme than Disney World. There's a story that when Walt Disney purchased the cheap swamp land in Orlando, he first held a huge party and invited everyone who would be a part of building the park. Electricians, plumbers, carpenters, welders, bulldozer operators, concrete layers, painters, designers, engineers and technicians all were included. An architectural firm built a model of the theme parks, and Walt had it displayed at the cook-out so workers could see the dream they were building. His desire was that workers would devote not only their labor to the project, but also their hearts.

Soon after the completion of Disney World, someone said, "Isn't it too bad that Walt Disney didn't live to see this?" Mike Vance, creative director of Disney Studios replied, "He did see it–that's why it's here." People need to dream more and learn to instill their dreams in others. When you stop dreaming, you start dying. Let your uninhibited creative juices flow and dream a little. Catch the vision that God has for you as His child. Dream of a place called heaven where there will be no pain, hate, sorrow, or tears–a place of joy, love, peace, and eternity with your Savior. Be a member of the "Dream Team!"

★ ★ ★

Further Study: What is your biggest dream? Do you share your dreams with others? What stops you from sharing your dreams? Take a 30 minute walk alone this week to dream a little.

HECATOMB

*Even if I am being poured out as a drink offering upon
the sacrifice and service of your faith.*
Philippians 2:17

★ ★ ★

Father Maximilian Kolbe was a prisoner at Auschwitz in August,
1941. Another prisoner escaped from the camp, and in reprisal, the Nazis
ordered 10 prisoners to die by starvation. Father Kolbe offered to take the
place of one of the condemned men. The Nazis kept Kolbe in the starvation bunker for two solid weeks and then put him to death by lethal injec-
tion on August 14, 1941. Thirty years later, a survivor of Aushwitz
described the effect of Father Kolbe's sacrificial action:

It was an enormous shock to the whole camp. We realized that someone among us in the spiritual dark night of the soul was raising the standard of life on high. Someone unknown, like everyone else, tortured and
bereft of name and social standing, went to a horrible death for the sake of
someone not even related to him. Therefore it is not true, we cried, that
humanity is cast down and trampled in the mud, overcome by oppressors,
and overwhelmed by hopelessness. Thousands of prisoners were con-
vinced the true world continued to exist and that our torturers would not
be able to destroy it. To say that Father Kolbe died for us or for that person's family is too great a simplification. His death was the salvation of
thousands. We were stunned by his act, which became for us a mighty
explosion of light in the dark camp.

What an incredible story of self-denial. How our world marvels at
such an act of sacrifice. What an impact it would make on you and I to
exemplify such sacrificial love for those with whom we have no relation.
Jesus started the way for us to follow. It's easy to sacrifice for those we love,
but how about those we don't care for or don't even know? Sacrifice with
no recognition is only done by divine intervention.

★ ★ ★

Further Study: What is the biggest sacrifice you ever made? When did you
do this? What does hecatomb mean? (Look it up.) What is the greatest
example of sacrifice you've ever seen or heard of?

JOKE'S ON THEM

We are fools for Christ's sake, but you are prudent in Christ; we are weak, but you are strong; you are distinguished, but we are without honor.
1 Corinthians 4:10

★ ★ ★

I know you've been on one end or the other of this beast before. What might we be talking about here? Look what day it is. Either you are planning or permitting (probably not by choice) a joke for today, and you may not even know you are the victim. If you are the culprit, be nice and do not embarrass the receiver. If you are the receiver . . . take cover. Far too many times it seems that the good guys always lose in this scene, and the bad guys (not really bad) are the ones riding off into the sunset grinning on their trusty horse.

All too often as Christians we appear, from our perspective, as the ones who look the fool in so many cases. Not cheating on a test when everyone else is, not chiming in on a gossip session, not going places we know will get us in trouble, not taking what is being stolen, not acting on a date like what seems to be the norm, and obeying our parents on curfew times, all can get us ridiculed. I'm sure nine out of 10 times the secular world looks at all this Christian commitment and just snickers like the roadrunner after a Wile Coyote flub. We may look like fools today, friend, but we're not living for the moment; we're living for the kingdom to come. Take notice, and notes (if you must), and realize that your Savior Jesus looked like a fool, too. He came into the world in a barn and went out on a mountain of trash called Calvary while hanging on a cross. Guess what? He also ascended into heaven to prepare our beds in His house for our coming . . . now, that's what I call a happy ending.

★ ★ ★

Further Study: When did the world last view you as a fool for Christ? How are you gonna' be seen today?

LOSING YOUR SHELL

"Have faith in God," Jesus answered.
Mark 11:22

★ ★ ★

From time to time a lobster (you know the red creatures with clamps for hands) leaves its shell as part of the growth process. The shell means protection, but when the lobster grows, the shell must be abandoned; otherwise, it would soon become a prison, and eventually a casket. The tricky part for the lobster is the period of time between discarding the old shell and forming the new one. During this vulnerable time, the lobster must be scared to death, as the ocean floor currents cartwheel it from coral to kelp. Hungry schools of fish are ready to make it a part of their dinner. For a while at least, the old shell must look pretty good—even if it had begun to feel a little like a girdle. Sometimes the unfortunate lobster dies between shells, but perhaps that's not as bad as suffocating in a shell that no longer fits. So it is with the life of a growing lobster in the ocean blue.

We aren't much different when it comes to growth. If we didn't have a shell (structure and framework) within which to grow, then I doubt if any of us would have made it this far. Even so, change and growth (maturity) are necessary for survival as a Christian. We don't often see the value at the time of change because it forces us out of our comfort zone and into our faith zone. The only way maturity can take place is to step out into faith and away from security and comfort. Discipleship means being so committed to Jesus that when He asks us to follow Him, to change, to ditch the security and comfort for a ride on faith, to risk it all, to grow, to leave our shells behind and be vulnerable and naked in a tough old world, we answer, "I'm yours, Lord!" Be prepared for anxious (up-tight) moments, fear, doubts, strange looks, and skepticism from others. You know . . . faith doesn't always make sense, but it doesn't have to.

★ ★ ★

Further Study: What is your shell (i.e. comfort zone, security, stronghold)? Why does God call you to leave your shell and become vulnerable? Is that comfortable? Why not? Why are change and maturity two key ingredients to spiritual growth?

BEING DEFINED

Since you died with Christ to the basic principles of this world, why,
as though you still belonged to it, do you submit to its rules.
Colossians 2:20

★ ★ ★

To be defined means to be calculated and prescribed for a stated meaning or purpose. I've never been one to spend free time reading the dictionary, but this thick book contains the meaning of every word in the English language. Even if you never knew a word existed, you'll find it in good old Webster's.

Our society defines thoughts, beliefs, theories and standards through the avenues of music, radio, television, newspapers and magazines. Billions of dollars are made each year by exploiting viewers and readers. These media vessels have also clued in that they can teach and mold a generation's way of thinking. What was considered vulgar and pornographic 30 years ago is now acceptable. Sex, violence, homosexuality, abortion, extramarital activity and a long list of other things can be seen on prime-time TV, or in million-subscriber magazines. Best selling books and albums (music) are at the top, not because of their brilliance, but because of their corrupt content. Why? We have been trained to listen to, read and watch things that are appealing to our flesh. Pigs love to wallow in the mud and so does a culture living in sin. We must stop defining ourselves and let God, through His Word, remold and re-program our way of thinking. These worldly vessels (media) should be down-right offensive to our spirits and repulsive to our minds. Stop it! Stop letting some guru at the controls of TV, record labels, publishing and so on, define your convictions. Take an active stand against such evils and boycott what's not right. Don't go to bad movies, don't buy CD's that have negative lyrics, don't buy pornographic publications, don't subscribe to liberal newspapers. No, you won't put them out of business, but you will not help fund their efforts, and that is doing something about it.

★ ★ ★

Further Study: Do you feel you are exploited by the media in any way? Are your thoughts, beliefs, and standards being defined by them? What should be defining you? How can you be redefined?

THE HEAT IS ON

And don't be conformed to this world, but be transformed by the renewing
of your mind, that you may prove what the will of God is,
that which is good and acceptable and perfect.
Romans 12:2

★ ★ ★

Can you feel it? It starts with a few butterflies, graduates to sweat, then comes in the form of a knot deep in the pit of your stomach and finally climaxes with short breaths and tight muscles. What is this disease we are talking about? Pressure. It comes in all shapes and sizes and doesn't choose favorites for its victims. We find it around every corner of our lives. Through sports, education, business, medical fields, families and friends, we feel it. One way or another, sometime in your life, you will meet this beast, and you'll either defeat the foe or become clutched in its painful jaws. Pressure is something we all wish we could avoid, but when encountered and victoriously conquered, we realize the process feels better than winning any championship or earning any "A." Realizing that pressure can be a verb, not just a noun and is a state mind, is winning half the battle.

When God created the heavens and the earth, there probably weren't too many pressures that existed other than volcanic. That is until people were painted into the picture. He knew that people would pressure others into situations they wished had never existed. We call it "peer" pressure, but I call it "conforming" pressure. Nobody turns the heat up in our lives to conform to another image worse than friends. True friendship is a sacrificial love, not a conditional one. You were created in God's image, not the world's, and you do live in the world, but you're not of the world cuz' you're a new creature, remember? The best and only way to defeat the pest of pressure is to exterminate with God's purifying Word daily.

Not too long ago Michael Jordan did a commercial that was really fun for Gatorade (which I love to drink), and the slogan was "Be like Mike!" With no disrespect to Michael, I personally think I'll keep trying to be like Christ. It may not allow you to dunk, but it will win you victory in life.

★ ★ ★

Further Study: What pressure do you face today? How are you going to defeat it?

99

T.G.I.F.

God demonstrated His own love for us, in that while
we were still sinners, Christ died for us (you).
Romans 5:8

★ ★ ★

We hear it all the time . . . T.G.I.F. . . . . thank God it's Friday! Most folks throw this term around like a monkey does a banana peel and don't have a clue what it really means. Most use it without any reverence to or for God, and they are just bustin' at the seams because it signals the last of the work week. It allows folks to go ballistic for two days each week when they can relax, play, take a nap, and basically just "do their own thing." The Friday before Easter, you know chocolate bunnies and sugar eggs, is called Good Friday. It's a day where millions of believers in Christ all over this planet are mindful of what God did for them through Christ, His Son, 2,000 years previously. Why is it so good, when it marks a dreadful day when a blameless lamb was sent to slaughter on a cross at Calvary for you and me? That sure doesn't sound like my definition of good by any stretch of the imagination. Sounds more like a "day that Jesus went down in defeat" than it does a day we should celebrate each year.

The apostle Paul gives us the answer in an nutshell. The love here is too profound for any Einstein to grasp, yet so simple that any little child could accept. No doubt, T.G.I.F. by all means. This truly is a day which sets the tone for a happy Easter and excitement to be worshipping a living (not dead) God. Next time you hear the disc jockey on the radio use that phrase, T.G.I.F., maybe you can be thankful for one particular Friday in history . . . it will bring more joy than finding some old hard-boiled egg, I bet.

★ ★ ★

Further Study: What is the significance in Good Friday to a Christian? What does Easter mean to you? How can this one Friday in history change someone's life? Why do other religion's worship a dead god? How cool is it that Jesus is alive today?

UNDERDOG

Encourage one another day after day as long as it's still called today
lest your heart be hardened by the deceitfulness of sin.
Hebrews 3:13

★ ★ ★

The Nickelodeon channel has a cartoon on each Sunday morning that is a stitch. This goofy little dog in a superman outfit comes out and says, "There's no need to fear, Underdog is here," then flies off to fight crime on the streets. I've personally always been the type to root for the person or team who is supposed to lose. Somebody once asked President Eisenhower why he ever bought that farm of his located in Gettysburg, Pennsylvania. He told them that all of his life he wanted to take a piece of ground which really hadn't been cared for (cultivated or fertilized or watered) and work with everything he had to leave it in better condition than he found it, and that's exactly what he did.

You know, that is such a simple principle, yet it is loaded with truth. Many folks in life, regardless of what they do or where they're from, have that inner urge to make a winner out of a loser. We are always looking for a big challenge, and there is really none too big with God as our source of power and motivation. William Barclay wrote, "One of the highest duties is to encourage others . . . it is easy to laugh at men's ideals; it is easy to pour cold water on their enthusiasm; it is easy to discourage. The world is full of discouragers. We have a Christian duty to encourage one another. Many a time a word of praise or thanks or appreciation or cheer has kept a man on his feet. Blessed is the man who speaks such a word."

Jesus was the underdog by the world's standards yet became the victor and now sits at the throne of God. With a simple wink of an eye, smile, soft word or serving hand, you can encourage someone to be or do better and follow Christ's example. Don't expect a lot of praise or to sign any autographs for encouraging others because it's definitely not the norm. Don't be one of those folks in life who rains on everyone else's parade . . . be there with ticker-tape and banners waving high for encouragement.

★ ★ ★

Further Study: Do you ever feel like an underdog? How do you treat the world's underdogs? Are Christians really the underdogs, or ultimate victors?

101

PODS

If any widow has children, let them learn to practice piety in regard to their own family, and make some return to their parents for this is good in God's eyes.

1 Timothy 5:4

★ ★ ★

Recently, I was watching one of those educational shows which come on late Sunday evenings. This particular show was a documentary on those zany creatures of the sea (no, not the Little Mermaid), the killer whale. These enormous conglomerations of blubber, fins and teeth have intrigued me since I visited Sea World in Florida and got spit on by Shamu. I did learn though, that these predators of the sea seem to have the personality of a puppy and the family standards we ought to have. Their family is correctly called a "pod," and they stay together at all times. Starting at the moment of birth, the calf (baby whale) and its mommy will always breath in unison . . . the mom surfaces for air at the same time as her young. The families of whales can be as large as 50 and stay together until death. They hunt, swim, play and learn from each other throughout their life-span. So, the next time you see one at an aquarium, look past the flips and stunts and notice the loyalty that runs deeper than any ocean.

We've lost the art of "pod" making. In human terms, we don't value the family unit like we should and God intended. Our number one focus here on earth is to build a structure (like the three little pigs) that can't be blown down by the wolves of time. Alcohol, divorce, drugs, anger, rebellion and sex outside marriage are a few weapons of wind the wolves huff and puff to try to blow down our homes. To change the trends we have got to put a huge value on the family fortress and never give in to the armies of hell. Satan would like nothing more than to destroy our lives through a dysfunctional family. A family needs to be a refuge, haven, security blanket and living quarters of love, therein serving its chosen purpose. We need to take a lesson from the untainted lifestyle of the killer whales of the sea and get our family back swimming together. Realize that Christ is and will have to be the glue which holds your pod together. Begin by eating one meal a day, praying one time a day, serving once a week and encouraging once an hour.

★ ★ ★

Further Study: What is your definition of a family? Does it jive with the biblical one? Are you glue in your home? How?

JESUS THE C.E.O.

In everything you do put God first, and He will direct
you and crown your efforts with success.
Proverbs 3:6

★ ★ ★

Okay, here's a wacked-out thought for you to compute in your cranium. Can you imagine if Jesus came back to earth today dressed not in a cloak and sandals, but in pinstripes and wingtips? What if He drove a Lexus downtown to a sizable skyscraper and took over as "the boss" (Chief Executive Officer) of a major investment firm on Wall Street? Could He succeed? Let's just see . . . in only three short years Jesus defined a mission and formed strategies to carry it out to completion. He had a small staff of 12 unlikely, unqualified, unruly disciples. With that staff He organized Christianity, which today has branches in all corners of the world and a 32.4% share of the population–twice the size of the closest rival's. His salesmen (disciples) took all they learned and utilized it in everyday life. Jesus (the marketing master) developed original material to market eternity to a broad-based region of purchasers. His salesmen learned sizzlin' sales-pitches like salvation, love, joy, healing, heaven and guaranteed success.

I think it would be interesting to compare today's tycoons' self-help strategies with Christ's divine one-liners. Catch this idea–if people in the corporate world would review the real book of success (the Bible), I think they might learn something. (scripture is, was and always will be a landmark for you and I, no matter what career path we choose.) Don't slough off that thick, dusty, unused book on the piano (the Bible) as just a fable of fiction, value it as words of wisdom. Jesus' way to climb the corporate ladder might surprise you.

★ ★ ★

Further Study: Ask your father (or any business man) what his secret to success is, then compare that with Matthew 5:1-10.

UNDER THE SEA

He rebuked the wind and the surging waves of the sea,
and it became perfectly calm.
Mark 4:39

★ ★ ★

My feelings on the subject of scuba diving are pretty simple . . . if God wanted us to breath underwater, He would have given us gills. It was totally against my better judgment to try my hand at this sport, but peer pressure overtook me. I first had to go through the difficult procedure of obtaining a license and certification, which I thought was enough. After graduating from scuba school, I was then permitted in the big pool–the ocean. Open water is a lot more different than a pool or lake. Why? 'Cuz there are animals that don't take kindly to us blowfish humans trespassing on their territory. We paid our fee, loaded the giant scuba boat and drifted out to sea. We headed out to a reef that was home to all kinds of marine life, including sharks (I'd be happier with "Flipper"). The boat tossed around like the S.S. Minnow, and I'd swear the crew included Gilligan and the Skipper. Talk about motion sickness (better known as ocean sickness while at sea). I'd never seen waves 20-feet tall or that rough. That all changed once we strapped on our gear and took the Nestea plunge.

The surface seemed out of control, yet below it was calm, quiet, and peaceful. Amazing . . . how could it be so bad from one perspective and so peaceful from another? It's a lot like God's perspective. We see the craziness, yet God sees the peace. He controls both sides, but from a human's vantage we think God has left us. The turbulent waters that Jesus and Peter walked on were calm below the surface. No matter how tough life may seem, God keeps it all under control if we only dive into the divine. God never leaves us; we leave Him. God's faithfulness is always just a prayer away. We have not (His peacefulness) because we ask not. Dive in!

★ ★ ★

Further Study: How peaceful is your life? How much peace do you have in the midst of turbulent trials? How much do you seek God's peace in the midst of your trials?

LAMP LIGHTER

Thy word is a lamp unto my feet and a light unto my path.
Psalm 119:105

★ ★ ★

When most of us hear this verse, we immediately recall Amy Grant singing the song. You've heard if for years in church, youth groups and on the radio, but have you ever stopped and looked at it? It comes off as a pretty simple set of divine words which have a nice ring to them, and they fit well with musical notes. Read it one time through, and your report would be that the Bible is like a light to my steps along this Christian journey, right? Well, pretty close, but look again . . . notice a key word in this verse? No, it's not lamp or light, but "feet." Check this bad boy thought out for a minute. God's word is a light, but its halo only surrounds your steps. Get it? Okay, I'll explain further . . . when you are walking down a narrow path at night with a flashlight pointed downward, you can only see a few feet (no pun intended) ahead of you at a time. In other words, you still need to walk with care (slowly, one step at a time) or you'll run into a tree, or stumble on an unnoticed boulder. I mean, if God wanted to, He could light up the country side with His word so you wouldn't even need a lamp. Come on now, this is God who can do it all, right?

The Bible is the flame in the lamp that gives light to every step our feet walk on this thin, windy pathway we call Christianity. I believe God is telling us that hey, the Bible is great, but it's not enough to make this journey . . . we still need His Spirit to guide us, too. He's telling us we must still carry faith in the Father accompanied by a lamp (not a spotlight) to find our way through life's dark, messed-up world in which we all travel. Study the Word of God daily to keep that flame from going out, and also keep the faith which compliments His word. Don't be afraid of the danger which will lie   ahead . . . you forget, Jesus made the path and has been on it several times before you.

★ ★ ★

Further Study: How often do you read the Bible? Do you believe it is a lamp to your feet? How can you get excited about God's Word? How can you make Bible study a habit?

CALLED TO ACCOUNT

*Now we know what the law says; it speaks to those under the law, that every
mouth may be closed and the world may be held accountable to God.*
Romans 3:19

★ ★ ★

This word will not come up in casual conversation at dinner. It won't appear on the prime time nightly news. It's not a category on the popular game show Jeopardy. You'll have to run with a different pack of folks to even use this word, yet it's essential to the survival of a concrete Christian today. What is this word? Accountability. The old dictionary defines it as "liable to be called to account for your action(s); responsible; capable of being explained."

About three years ago I realized at a ripe age of 32, how weak I was alone in my walk with Christ (I learn quickly, don't I?). The older I get, the less confidence I seem to have in myself for fighting this battle called faith, alone. Late one night I was watching one of those educational television shows on the Discovery channel, and I saw how packs of wolves would patiently wait until their prey, a thousand pound caribou crossing the frozen terrain of northern Canada, would file off alone. It was at that moment, like the wolves knew they were on camera, that they would charge the victim, like bugs to a light and take it down suddenly, without remorse. What a scene to show on the tube (I bet the animal rights folks were ticked). How sudden, how pre-planned, what violence, yet how true even in our own lives. Satan is the wolf (dressed in disguise) who waits for us to single ourselves away from the fellowship of other believers in the herd and bites to kill. Accountability keeps us out of the jaws of consumption and into the fearless hands of our Father in heaven. We are first called to be held accountable to God then to our agape friends daily. Accountability means having someone ask you the tough questions which matter in our walk with Christ. We need someone to not let us slack off and hold us to a standard we can't always hold ourselves to. Try it . . . I promise it's better than being prey in the jaws of sin.

★ ★ ★

Further Study: Who can hold you accountable today? How will you be consistent? When will you start?

SETBACK BE A COMEBACK

Fixing our eyes on Christ, the author and perfector of our faith.
Hebrews 12:2

★ ★ ★

Eamonn Coghlan was the Irish world record holder at 1,500 meters and was running in a qualifying heat at the World Indoor Track and Field Championships in Indianapolis, Indiana. With two and a half laps left in the race, he was accidentally tripped and fell to the track surface. Eamonn didn't get to be a record holder by having a quitter's attitude, so he pulled himself up to his feet, and with incredible effort, managed to catch up to the leaders in the race. With approximately 20 yards left to the finish line, he was in third place–good enough to qualify for the finals. Eamonn looked over his left shoulder and saw no one even close to him, so he let up to coast the last 10 yards. What he hadn't seen was a runner charging up over his right shoulder with the momentum to pass him at the finish line, thus eliminating him from the finals. His great comeback after a fall was rendered worthless by taking his eyes and heart off the finish line.

In today's world of chaos and fast lanes, it's tempting to let up when it looks like things around us are favorable. We feel comfortable the way we are and the way life is going for us, so we coast. We take it out of four-wheel drive and put it in neutral. The problem comes when our wheels begin to slip, we lose our momentum, and risk losing the race. I have always admired those few individuals that finish the race as excited and determined as when they started. Be the runner on God's track team that stays focused on the goal, purpose and reason (Jesus). You may get tripped up during this race, so have the mind-set going into it that you will not quit and you will get up. Make a set-back be a comeback.

★ ★ ★

Further Study: What conditions cause you to take your eyes off Christ? When are you tempted to just coast instead of press on? How can you become the type of Christian that finishes as strong as you start?

This New Age

Let no one be found among you who practices divination or sorcery, interprets omens, engages in witchcraft or one who casts spells, or who is a medium, or spiritist, or who consults the dead. Anyone who does these things is detestable to the Lord.
Deuteronomy 18:9-12

★ ★ ★

I heard a saying one time that said, "If you don't know where you're going, you'll probably get there." Our world is falling all over itself with people going nowhere. Daily you can read about someone on this planet who tries his/her hand at being or coming up with a new way of doing things. The New Age Movement is a rapidly growing cult of followers who at first glance seem to have the winning ticket for happiness. Words spill from their mouths like psychic, Nirvana, astrology, self-realization, reincarnation, pantheism, out-of-body experiences, transformation, channeling, ESP, karma and Shirley MacLaine. They practice their religion with tools such as crystals, yoga, ESP, Ouigi boards and tarot cards. The reason this cult has taken off like a bullet out of a barrel is it requires no sacrifice at all, and it's a tremendous self-image builder. Their doctrine is "if everything is god, then I am god."

The movement is all about no higher moral absolutes and that truth is perceived individually. The New Age Movement derides the biblical doctrine of sin and substitutes reincarnation as the means of atonement. They believe there is no reality; therefore, all deaths lead to another life on earth in another form (who knows, maybe you'll return as a cockroach).

Realize that this is one of many types of cults in today's world, and they all are dangerous to tangle with. You'll see where Christians have retreated in society (i.e. Hollywood, politics, music, etc.) as this movement has advanced. The goal of new agers is to change "how I feel" (it's all a feeling). How can we help in throwing a wrench in its gears? First, pray. Then, be a light in a dark world. Love your enemy. And finally, wear your armor daily (time in the Word).

★ ★ ★

Further Study: Have you been approached or seen this movement in your community? How can you better prepare yourself today for this battle?

HUMAN BEING OR HUMAN

The Lord God formed the man from the dust of the ground and breathed into his nostrils the breath of life, and the man became a human being.
Genesis 2:7

★ ★ ★

One of the greatest books of the Bible lies within the first several pages where God shows off His awesome power and creativity. When we read the book of beginnings, God seems to show us how all this began. When God created you He intended you to be in a relationship with Him from day one. There is a reason we were made human beings and not human doings. A human being what? In love with its Creator! Yep, you read it right, a human selling out his heart and soul to the Master mechanic of two-legged folks. Our greatest commandment that Moses brought back from the mountain is to "love the Lord God with all your heart, soul and mind." It seems like in this day and time, we tend to think we can actually pay God off with cheap works (doings) to get us to, or keep us in, those golden gates called heaven.

We are a society saved by grace, not by works (Ephesians 2:5). The word grace means to stoop or bow. You cannot earn the right to go to heaven, just accept the ticket (salvation through Christ) and say "thank you" for the cross of calvary. My dad is a horse rancher. For years I have watched him walk stooped-over across a pasture, never standing higher than the horse, right up to a newborn colt, who has never seen a human before, and begin to rub and pet this colt. The colt doesn't run away. Why? Because my dad humbly stoops (with grace) in order not to intimidate the baby colt by his size or stature.

Take this to the bank and deposit it. You are called first to love God and develop a relationship, then the fruits of faith will follow. Try being what you were created to do and that's "be."

★ ★ ★

Further Study: How intimate is your relationship to the Creator? How can it be better?

TICKED OFF

Be angry, and yet do not sin; do not let the sun go down on your anger.
Ephesians 4:26

★ ★ ★

Have you ever had any of the following thoughts before? It's a sin to get angry. Don't share your angry feelings with anyone. God doesn't understand anger. Hold all anger inside. The best way to deal with anger is to ignore it. Jesus never got angry. Anger is only an outward feeling. Anger shows spiritual immaturity. God doesn't forgive anger. Christians just don't get angry.

Well, if you chimed right in on this "top 10" list, then listen up because what you see is not necessarily what you get. In this day and time, it's easy to get ticked off when you've been done wrong: cut off by another car, butted in front of in the checkout line, called something you're not, felt like you've been dealt a bad hand in the game of life. Jesus Himself felt these same emotions 2,000 years ago. A common Bible story tells how an angry Jesus turned over mega tables set up by tax collectors in His Father's temple. What about Mark 3:5 or John 3:36? These recorded instances were true expressions of anger by our Savior, and when looked intently upon, equate to a slow rising type of anger in which Jesus is displeased with the situation, but handles it like it should be handled, without violence or destruction. There are two types of anger (news to me) that are defined, one which is Christ-like, the other which is man-made. One is targeted at the disobedience and defiance of God's word, and the other contains jealousy and bitterness (Galatians).

You see, anger, handled as Jesus did, is not wrong if its pure motive is to correct and set back on the right path to Christ. The other is purely of the world and results in violence and uncontrolled outbursts that stem from desires of the flesh. Make it a point to check the reason behind your anger first, then deal with it directly in accordance to scripture before the sun goes down that day.

★ ★ ★

Further Study: What ticks you off the most? Why?

THE HUNT

*So the other disciple who had first come to the tomb entered
then also, and he saw and believed.*
John 20:8

★ ★ ★

I wasn't quite sure if I was attending a concert or an early morning
Easter service. The location was "Fiddler's Green," and the attendance was
somewhere around 10,000. It was an outdoor amphitheater, and you
couldn't have painted a more beautiful day or a more scenic backdrop than
the Colorado Rockies (and I don't mean the baseball team). I was amazed
at the number that showed up, yet I question some motivations for attendance. Did they come because of ritual, guilt, status or conviction, or was
it for celebration? Well . . . only God knows, but the worship service was
awesome.

Easter is far more than a time to hunt for colored, hard-boiled eggs or
dress up in a festive new outfit. It's above all the hype, yet down to earth
enough to understand. Easter is the celebration following Good Friday
which separates Christianity from many other religions. You see those who
worship another god honor a dead god that didn't die specifically for
them. We get so excited about the empty tomb, because our future lies in
a risen Lord. When Peter and the other disciples saw the empty tomb,
they realized what Mary knew as she sat outside the tomb and wept. As
believers in Christ, we don't worship a grave, bronze statue or a past legend, but a risen, living, breathing, omnipresent God. Now, if that thought
doesn't get your blood flow movin', then I'm not sure you are alive (take a
moment and check your pulse). Gang, who gives a rip about the tomb?
He's alive!

★ ★ ★

Further Study: Why should you be more excited about a living Jesus than
an empty tomb? Why is it so important to our faith that we worship and
follow a L-I-V-I-N-G Savior?

EXTENSION

Which one of you by worrying can add a single cubit to his life?
Matthew 6:27

★ ★ ★

Jane Fonda, Richard Simmons, Kathy Smith, Cindy Crawford and Bruce Jenner have all made thousands of dollars selling not only machines or techniques, but a false concept. Info-commercials are packed with trim and tight, fit and fancy, sexy and skinny models peddling products like Nordic-Trac, Ab-roller, Life-cycle, Gut-buster or Thigh-Master. Health clubs are packed with exercise fanatics with one goal in mind, to look good and feel good with the hope of living longer. Hear me out here, I am not down on anyone or any product, but I am down on the concept of extending one's life through the vehicle of workouts and exercise. scripture is very direct and clear that your body is the temple of our Lord. I personally believe our Savior shouldn't have to live in the ghetto (1 Corinthians 6:19). The serious issue here is trying to play god and actually thinking for one second that by weightlifting, aerobics, stair masters, stationary bikes, jogging, swimming or whatever you can actually add a few more years (cubits) to your life. God is in charge of our life expectancy (James 4:14), and when He says it's time to go (die) . . . you're gone! God invented time; even though health studies show the average American lives to be 75, there are no guarantees. In the above scripture, I think Jesus is saying, "Your destiny lies on your choosing Me or not choosing Me." A cubit is a measurement in Jesus' culture which was from the end of your elbow to the tip of your middle finger; now that varied a bit, but it equated to be around 18 inches. Isn't that a sarcastic comment when Jesus says, "Which one of you by worrying can add a single cubit to his life?" So, next time your "sweatin' to the oldies" or working on those "buns of steel," do it to enhance your quality of life . . . not quantity of years. Sweat on!

★ ★ ★

Further Study: Do you exercise? Why? What is the "real" reason to exercise?

DOULOS: A BOND SERVANT

*If you point these things out to the brothers, you will be a good minister
of Christ Jesus, brought up in the truths of faith and of the
good teaching that you have followed.*
1 Timothy 4:6

★ ★ ★

In the summer of 1989, Mark Wellman, a paraplegic, gained national recognition by climbing the sheer granite face of "El Capitan" in Yosemite National Park. On the seventh and final day of his heroic climb, the headline of the Fresno newspaper read, "Showing a Will of Granite." Mark's partner, Mike Corbett, who is not paralyzed, received little recognition. With the article was a picture of Mike carrying his companion on his shoulders, subtitled, "Paraplegic and partner prove no wall is too high to scale." The ironic thing about this event is that Mike scaled (climbed) the granite face of El Capitan three times in order to help Mark pull himself up once.

You won't find many articles, pictures, broadcasts or praise going out for a servant. You don't see people flocking around a servant, badgering him for an autograph. To be a servant means to serve when you're not cast in the lead role (the star). Servanthood is a lost art. To be a servant is to exemplify humility and selflessness in its truest form (be like Christ). No standing ovations or syndicated TV shows await a humble servant. In fact, servants are looked upon as the lowest member of the food chain. A Doulos (bond-servant) is as low as a snake's belly, seldom recognized, promoted, or viewed very highly by anyone . . . except God Almighty! God will (not might) exalt you over any mountain (like El Capitan) when you serve others. Serving reveals the Savior. Without it, you'll never accomplish great things for God's Kingdom.

★ ★ ★

Further Study: Are you a server or a servee? Do you think serving means giving or getting? Why do you see few Doulos bond-servants in society today? Why do you think Jesus asks you to be one? Will you? Why or why not?

FLY AWAY HOME

Each man should give what he has decided in his heart to give, not
reluctantly or under compulsion, for God loves a cheerful giver.
2 Corinthians 9:7

★ ★ ★

Birds of the air are interesting to watch. Now, I don't I consider myself a real bird watcher, but you can learn a lot from them. There is a lesson in watching a swallow teach its young to fly. The mother bird gets the chicks out of the nest, high atop a tree and starts shoving them out toward the end of the branch. Before the chicks do a nose-dive into the pavement, they learn to fly. If a chick tightens its talons (claws) on the branch and refuses to jump, the mother will peck at its feet. When the chick can't stand the pain anymore, it lets go and flies. Birds have feet and can walk, talons that can grasp a tree branch tightly, but flying is their heritage. Not until they fly are they living at their best and doing what they were intended to do.

You know, giving is what Christians do best. It is the air into which we were born. It is the action that was designed into us before our birth, yet sometimes we desperately try to hold on and live for self. We look bedraggled and pathetic doing it, hanging on to the dead branch of a bank account, afraid to risk ourselves on the untried wings of giving. We don't think we can live generously because we've never tried it before. The sooner we start, the quicker we find the joy that accompanies giving and letting go for God. God will peck at the closed hands of our heart until we stop feeling, or let go and let God work. Flying is more fun than watching anyway.

★ ★ ★

Further Study: Are you a giver? To what do you give? Are you a hoarder? Why? Did you come into this world with money? Are you gonna' leave this world with money? How can you become a better giver?

A LEARNED TRAIT

For I have learned to be content in all circumstances.
Philippians 4:11

★ ★ ★

One of the hottest behind-the-counter drugs that Americans use today is Valium. It's kind of a mind tranquilizer that allows oneself to have the attitude of "let well enough alone." Call it what you want, take your pick of adjectives like complacent, peaceful, satisfied, at ease, sans souci, not particular, resigned, unaffected, serene, unmolested, comfortable (tired yet?) or unperturbed (whatever). We have a tendency in our terrain to always be wanting on the other side of the fence. The reason that we pop Valium in our diet is the pressure to escape our present situation. Why is it that we're always looking for something better like the newest car, computer, job, house, lingo, style of clothes, hairstyle or spouse? What happened to loyalty and contentment with where we are at the moment? No, I'm not saying that we are not to strive for perfection or push ourselves, but come on . . . we've lost that balance. When it begins to be like a game of Monopoly where you're continually trying to get more and more, then there is a problem. The apostle Paul speaks louder than a tornado siren when he (of all people) states that he has become content in all things. I mean, this guy hasn't had much to brag about to his neighbors in a while. He has been beaten, blamed and posted bail for being a disciple of Jesus for years. His home has been a jail cell, his life persecuted and his body beaten to a pulp, and he says he is content no matter if he's in the club house or outhouse. We can learn a huge lesson in life . . . if we learn to be content in whatever circumstances our sovereign God has placed us. You know, if we could learn this lesson in God's classroom, we wouldn't need the school nurse for aspirin (or Valium) nearly as much. Then, our local drugstores could be selling more cold medicine than pain pills.

★ ★ ★

Further Study: What always makes you want to retreat from a situation? What exactly is contentment? How can you obtain more of it? Is contentment a way of thinking or a place we all come to?

SIRENS

His calamity will come suddenly, and instantly he will be broken.
Proverbs 6:15

★ ★ ★

Growing up in a big city, they were as normal as flies at a picnic, but now living in a small country town, they are as noticeable as a ketchup stain on a white shirt. I'm talking about the scream of sirens. When you hear one while in a car, you're supposed to pull over and give right of way, but when you're on a street corner, all you do is stop, look and wonder. Sirens only show up in our lives when something bad is in the process of happening. It may mean a fire, wreck, heart attack, shooting or funeral procession, but you can bet it's not for a birthday party. Usually the people who become directly involved with a siren are either scared, mesmerized, hysterical, crying, confused or just plain terrified. Count on it, you will hear one or more in due time with the direction our country is headed. The final destination of the siren won't be a chill-out moment in time. Rest assured that the folks involved need more than a fire hose or paramedics . . . they need God.

Whether you hear them as loudly as you do those on top of a police car or not, they are still there. Siren sounds come dressed in a little different shape and are presented in random packages. They may sound like an outburst of anger or a cutting remark. You may see them drunk or high at a party, or they may reveal themselves by leaving a 20-year marriage with a wife and two kids, but they are sirens. You see, sirens are nothing more than attitudes which emit actions as warning signals. You hear and see them far more than you do the flashing lights. We have become so callused to them we have grown accustomed to their ways and accept them as a "norm." False! Wrong   answer . . . we need to realize they are cries for help, and we need to be of assistance as much as we would if we were performing CPR. Be alert at all times for people sirens in your life. Be attentive to what is going on in the arenas in which you live. Be a useful hand of God to a world falling apart. And the next time you hear a siren, I hope your eyes and ears perk up like a dog's to a signal of help needed.

★ ★ ★

Further Study: What are the siren sounds you hear the most? How do your friends cry out for help? Are you willing to help?

BAD HABITS

*Do you not know that your body is a temple for the Holy Spirit
who is in you whom you have received from God?*
1 Corinthians 6:19

✶ ✶ ✶

The "he-man" rugged model for the macho nacho cigarette power-house, Marlboro, succumbed to cancer at age 51. You may remember him as the weathered cowboy, marked with tattoos and chapped lips, who rode the range punching cows like the men of the Old West. What he did for the manufacturer was lead consumers to believe the stud thing to do was to smoke. What we didn't see on the billboards was that he spent the last three years of his life warning others of the dangers of smoking. Though it was too late for him, he thought if he could keep just one youth from starting, or help one smoker to stop, it would all be worth it. He was a convincing spokesperson because he knew all too well the price to be paid for becoming enslaved to this habit. You'll never see a magazine ad or billboard poster showing a smoke-filled room of emaciated hackers throwing up their offerings to the god of tobacco. The lesson can be learned that all of us can be overtaken by a habit which owns our lives and body.

My personal belief is that if God intended us to smoke we would all be born with exhaust systems. Granted, this is just one of many bad habits that we bow down to. We are to worship no other god than the Creator of the universe. Another god could be classified as anything that takes jurisdiction in our lives and fights for the number one spot in our hearts. Bad habits develop simply from lack of self-control. Take control of those areas that have escaped from the corral and are now running wild in your life. Seek help from other supporting believers by confessing the habit and the need for their prayers and accountability. Don't forget there is a big God who loves you, and all He desires is to be asked for His help to make you more like His Son, then look out! Bad habits are like a comfortable couch, easy to get into and hard to get out of.

✶ ✶ ✶

Further Study: What bad habits do you have that have taken over in your life? Do you desire to quit? Do you want to quit badly enough to seek help? When are you gonna' start?

117

SOCIAL TRENDS

Glorify God in your body.
1 Corinthians 6:20

★ ★ ★

A trend is defined as a social movement or surge in a specific area in our culture. Noticed recently is the adornment trend of tattoos and piercing. It doesn't take an investigative journalist or a fashion consultant to see just how (no pun intended) ingrained these fashion statements have become. Crossing mono-sexual boundaries, these trends are now unisex. Tattoos show up on ankles, arms, hands and places too risky to discuss. Piercing takes place not only in the ears, but the naval, nose and lips. Such adornments are not a new idea to civilization, but the recoil of these trends is strong. It boils down to how can followers of Christ keep the balance? When is it proper to follow a trend?

Now, I realize that this is a controversial issue. I think scripture gives us the parameters to decide how Christians are to conduct themselves. The question one needs to ask is why? Why do I feel the need to partake in the trend? The answer may lie in individual insecurities, rebellion or expression of a particular image. On the other hand, the motive may be pure and undefiled. You need to do some soul searching and motive meddling to find the personal inner-answer for yourself. Ask yourself, no matter what the trend of the year is:

Why am I participating? (Motive)
What does scripture say about it? (Means)
What would Jesus do? (Mentor)
Who am I honoring? (Method)

Now, rely on the Holy Spirit and your conscience to direct your decision in the matter. Oh yeah, you probably noticed that I didn't really answer the question. You're right, Sherlock . . . that's because the decision is yours . . . I've already made mine.

★ ★ ★

Further Study: So how do you feel about these two issues? Are you participating in either of them now? Why or why not?

WINE PRESS

I now rejoice in my sufferings for you, and fill up that which is behind of the afflictions of Christ in my flesh for His body's sake.
Colossians 1:24

★ ★ ★

We continually strive for those mountain top experiences of life. Prior to conversion to Christ, you may have lived daily on the top, yet after this experience you learn a revolutionary lesson. God can allow life with Him to rivet us with pain that is more intense than anything we might have dreamed. One moment we are lost, then after a radiant flash, we see what He is really after and say, "Lord, here I am. Do what needs doing to make me more like you." This event has nothing to do with personal sanctification, but instead being made broken bread and poured-out wine. God can never make us into wine if we object to the fingers He uses to squeeze the grapes (you and me). If God would only use His own fingers, we would feel special. But when He uses someone we don't like or a set of difficult circumstances as the crushers, we hate it. We must never choose our own martyrdom (pain). If we want to be made into wine, we will be crushed because no one can drink grapes. Grapes only become wine when they're crushed.

If by chance the grapes of your spiritual walk are not ripe, then the wine would be bitter if God squeezed you. You have to be totally in tune with God before the squeezing and pouring-out process can take place. Keep your life "right" with God and let Him have His way with you, and you will see that He is producing the kind of bread and wine that will benefit His Kingdom. The older you get the sweeter the wine will become in life . . . you'll see.

★ ★ ★

Further Study: What kind of finger and thumb of God has been squeezing you? Why is pressure so important on the wine press? If you're not getting squeezed, then what do you see as the problem? When will you be ready?

119

SCARRED FOR LIFE

You have been bought with a price; don't be the servants of man.
1 Corinthians 7:23

★ ★ ★

If you're ever doing the "traveling thing" and your journey happens to take you across the western plains of Texas, you'll see tumbleweeds, windmills, miles of pasture, fields of bluebells, old postcard gas stations and the state bird of Texas–the cow. That's right, there are more of those lonesome doggies (cows) per square mile in the area around Hereford, Texas, than anywhere else in the world. You'll find every make of cow imaginable from Black Angus to the white-faced Hereford. In the late 1800s the cattle industry experienced a surge in what they commonly called, "cattle rustlin'," which was really just plain stealing. The thieves rustled up someone else's herd and took it to market to sell for themselves. With so many large herds of cattle coming in each day, it was difficult to identify one rancher's cow from the next. Little could be done to stop the thieves unless they were caught red-handed. That was true until the invention of the "branding iron," which permanently marked livestock with the custom brand of the owner's ranch name, like JH, T-Bar-M or Bar-K.

Believe it or not, you, as a follower of Christ, have been branded (spiritually, not physically). Remember that the brand symbolizes ownership and loyalty to a particular person and place of residence. As a Christian your owner (Jesus) paid the debt on the cross, and now your future pasture of peace is heaven. Isn't that cool, to think you are scarred with the mental brand of Calvary, setting you apart from the others you rub shoulders with every day? Be proud of your owner, yet humble to your position here on earth. The hot branding iron process that marked the rawhide of a cow was a painful procedure, but your pain was borne by your Savior. What a deal!

★ ★ ★

Further Study: What does being bought with a price say about Christ's love for you? Are you proud to be a member of the heavenly herd? How can you help others know about your future pasture?

PRAYER ON PROPOSAL

*For those things which you pray, believe that you have
received them, and they shall be given to you.*
Mark 11:24

★ ★ ★

Now this is not gonna' be one of those devotions on "name it, claim it." This devotion is on a kind of prayer warrior who has the right perspective and procedure. I'll begin with a true story I heard in a small farming community in western Iowa. As usual, the good ol' American farmer was being dealt another bad hand in the weather department. Not a drop of rain had fallen for a total of 31 days, so a town meeting was called. The location was the local church with the preacher presiding. The gathering was basically a prayer meeting to ask God to show favor on their dry, scorched farm land and crops so they could have a good harvest to pay some bills. The reason this meeting and story are so interesting is that all the locals who attended the meeting came with umbrellas. Now that's what I call an expectant prayer meeting.

We, as Christians, only have one road to travel to see the Savior, and that's on "Highway Prayer." The only communication we have with the Creator is through the two-way radio we call prayer. With all that in mind, isn't it important that we know how to pray? God will always answer your requests with either yes, no or wait. What we need to do more of is keep our tuner tuned to God so finely that our prayers match His way of thinking. This way, when we pray, we are so deeply into God's will and looking out for His best interest, all our requests and petitions are right on. Now what this does is give us the liberty to pray boldly through faith that we will receive His will for the particular situation we're praying for. Whether it's a need for healing someone sick, a material matter, guidance on a decision, or wisdom in our thinking, He will come through . . . bank on it.

So, be like that group of believers in Iowa and pray to God with results in mind . . . cuz' when it rains, it pours!

★ ★ ★

Further Study: Who or what can you pray for today? When you pray, do you pray believing God is listening? Do you pray consistently? Do you doubt you're righteous enough for God to listen?

HERO SHOPPING

Everyone, after he has been fully trained, will be like his teacher.
Luke 6:40

★ ★ ★

It doesn't take long in the riches of society to find poverty in the hero profession. The problem is that there are not many folks interviewing for this job because of the incredible amount of experience needed. One must be willing, honest, loyal, unselfish, humble, dedicated, caring, self-disciplined and intent on one purpose (I could go on). Wow! What a résumé would be needed in this job search. Isn't it funny that the profession we're talking about is the endangered species of real life, red, white and blue "heroes?" Isn't it ironic (look closely) that the qualities mentioned don't deal with head knowledge but heart knowledge? Believe it or not (no, it's not Ripley's), very few heroes or mentors are around to be followed. In this profession, the title must be earned; it's not just freely given. Worthiness must be proven on the playing fields of family relationships, battle grounds of business, spectrum of sports and the stadiums of society.

As you grow older, you will observe that trying to find this mentor is like trying to find a penny in the Grand Canyon. They come around about as often as a total eclipse of the sun, but guess what? They are out there in small numbers and not where you expect to see them. They carry no flash (they're humble); they wave not their own banner (unselfish), nor do they advertise their position (folks of integrity). The truth is, the position can only be held by a sincere follower of Jesus. Why? Without Him there is no divine strength to pull off walking upright day after day, year after year. If you want to find a hero, start first, not by looking for one, but by praying for one. God wants us all to have a mentor to teach us (like Paul did Timothy), and then wait on the Lord.

Let me offer a brief suggestion as you climb this mountain in search of a glimpse of this endangered species. See if they can say these simple, yet convicting words, "you can do as I do." Make sure they are an original and not a cheap replica of a real, live, modern day "hero."

★ ★ ★

Further Study: Who is your hero today? Can you do as they do? Is what they do honoring to God?

TURN DOWN THE VOLUME

Be still and know that I am God.
Psalm 46:10

★ ★ ★

In this civilization of chaos with so many living frantically on the fast track, few times in daily schedules could be classified as quiet, still times. Don't you feel like you're the hamster in the cage on a wheel going like mad, and you're on display for others to see? An article in the Boston newspaper tells how after Lenny Bias, first round draft choice of the Boston Celtics, was found dead of an overdose of cocaine, reporters questioned his high school coach, who said, "It looks like life in the fast lane got even faster." The pace of society doesn't exactly promote or applaud times of stillness and silence. Ever been in a conversation, or with a group of people, when all turned silent? Man, do the body languages start speaking, as heads start bowing, fingers and toes go to tapping with nervous gestures. Let's face up to it, we don't like quiet or the fact that we're still because we feel like time is passing us by without anything productive happening. Just the opposite is true to God. Be sure you don't let your feelings become fact in this situation.

God, being a caring Creator, doesn't want to try to speak above the volume of society. You and I both know when God needs to get our attention, He can. But He chooses not to, unless we want Him to. Learn, while you're young, to find a consistent quiet time daily in a specific location, which is like a secret hide-out that only you and the Savior know about. When you're at that spot and begin to read His word, study it. When you pray for guidance, listen to His answer. You can't do all this while on the treadmill of life. Who knows, you may begin to glow after meeting with God each day . . . Moses did.

★ ★ ★

Further Study: Did you find a still, quiet place today to visit with Jesus? Why not? How can you?

123

FLICKS

Your eyes will see strange things, and your mind will utter perverse things.
Proverbs 23:33

★ ★ ★

Summertime is definitely the bread-and-butter of Hollywood. According to *Movieguide* magazine there is a little different twist to the reports coming out of movie land. Despite Hollywood's insistence that it is making more movies for the American family, less than half of 1994's releases were rated acceptable for teenagers or for children. The report went something like this:

NC-17 rated movies	1%
G rated movies	3%
Not rated movies	14%
PG rated movies	19%
PG-13 rated movies	22%
R rated movies	41%

Now, there is no one who loves a good flick (movie) more than me. Buttered popcorn, 32-ounce soda pop, Junior Mints and Gummy Bears are as mandatory at a movie as hot dogs and soft pretzels are at a baseball game. The problem is the standards of the movie rating system. Violence, sex and offensive language are huge box office draws. You can't tell me you can watch a two-hour movie infected with nudity (or sexual connotations), excessive violence, and offensive language, and not be swayed by these brain-branding scenes. These impure movies are easily accessed at theaters, in hotel rooms, or on your home TV set. Whether you see it or not, your character, beliefs, standards and rationale is persuaded to agree with Hollywood's philosophies. Every time you buy a movie ticket, you are supporting the production of another movie. My plea to you is send a message to movie-land, loud and clear, that you are not (as a Christian) going to lower your integrity or standards to this filth any longer. You can't turn off your mind or shut your ears, so flee (run or avoid) from this junk. Next time you're watching a movie, ask yourself if Jesus were to appear in physical form next to you, would you still watch it?

★ ★ ★

Further Study: What rating do you go to? R? PG-13? Are PG movies free of sex, violence or offensive language? Are the movies you watch acceptable by Jesus' standards?

SEMESTER THINKING

To the pure, all things are pure.
Titus 1:15

★ ★ ★

The *Wall Street Journal* reports that in a recent study, one of the reasons the deadly virus HIV causes AIDS is because it is a tenacious opponent. An infected person produces a billion (that's right–billion) particles of the virus daily. This is a ton more than anyone had previously believed true. The body's immune system fends off many of these particles, but over time, it's overwhelmed by the attack. The disease's proclivity for mutation has been recognized for quite some time. This, together with the newly discovered productivity, caused a researcher named David Ho (director of the Aaron Diamond AIDS Research Center in New York where HIV's multiplying power was discovered) to state that no drug currently under testing can eradicate the virus in a patient. Even small amounts are capable of eventually producing mutants that can resist any drug. There may be little hope in the medical field, but there is in the spiritual field–purity.

Now, I realize that a percentage of people get this virus through impure blood transfusions, needles and odd means. I also know, however, that by and large, this deadly disease is transferred through sexual activity. AIDS is not going to be cured by man's hand, but from his heart. Purity is a word seldom heard in casual conversation, but found often in scripture. AIDS is, for the most part, a consequence of immorality. Yes, tons of Christians are cleansed mentally of immorality, but not from its physical consequence. Medical science hasn't created a condom for the conscience yet. Realize that what you do today can and will affect your tomorrow. Stop living your life in semesters, thinking that you can play around sexually now, and then settle down when you get older. God's grace is the only cure for this sickness. It starts by purifying our hearts, which leads to purity of our bodies.

★ ★ ★

Further Study: Does what you do now affect your future? How? Are you pure? Why does God tell us to live pure and undefiled lives?

125

THE IMMORAL MAJORITY

All will be condemned who have not believed the truth
but have delighted in wickedness.
2 Thessalonians 2:12

★ ★ ★

It was a news flash that stunned the world. Any international event took a back seat to the billion people who viewed the funeral at the 13th century church in London, England, on September 6, 1997. At 12:30 a.m. in Paris, after leaving dinner at the Ritz, the Princess of Wales, Lady Diana, and her wealthy boyfriend, Dodi al Fayed, jumped into a chauffeur-driven Mercedes and eight minutes later died in a sudden car crash.

Ironically, on the eve of the funeral, a friend of the princess, Mother Teresa of Calcutta, India, died of heart problems at the age of 87. Mother Teresa was called "mother to the poor" and felt called by God for life to minister to the poor, sick and needy on the streets of India. The media frenzy couldn't find any more room in their papers or on their broadcasts for her.

I truly believe that freedom of speech has been taken to the extreme and now dictates actions and attitudes. The media of today is a powerful, effective tool in the hands of darkness. My point is that most TV shows, magazines articles, radio broadcasts and newspaper columns come to you with a secular, humanistic slant. Mother Teresa once said, "I am a little pencil in the writing hand of God." The opposite can be said about this world's media avenues. In the Old Testament they had prophets, in the New Testament they had Jesus, and now you and I have God's Word and Spirit to guide us and teach us the truth. I truly believe that in a deceitful, lawless world, we need to cling to God's sovereignty and ways, not what we are getting fed by the media. Be careful what you take in as facts. Filter every word you hear or read through scripture and the Spirit of God who lives inside your heart and steers your mind, will and emotions. If you really think about it, the media situation is an important international moral problem; the media and press are fueled by the readers, watchers and listeners who have acquired a taste for immorality and continue to buy the junk and fuel the fire for the media to stay in business.

★ ★ ★

Further Study: How much media teaching do you take in daily? Do you screen what you watch, read and take as fact? How can you purify your heart and mind daily?

EXCESS BAGGAGE

For my iniquities have gone over my head; As a heavy
burden they weigh too much for me.
Psalm 38:4

★ ★ ★

It had been one of those days from the moment I got up at 7:00 a.m.
I nearly melted my eyebrows with a hair dryer, and my shirt had a giant
grape juice stain on the back. I was scheduled to be in Denver by 1:00 p.m.
for a connecting flight through Dallas/Ft. Worth Airport with a 35 minute
lay-over. I opted not to check any bags below the plane for fear the airlines
would pull a bonehead stunt and lose my luggage. My flight came in late
to Dallas, not to mention that I almost had to use the barf-bag, and I was
left with about 10 minutes to catch the Denver plane five miles from the
place where we'd arrived. I ran down the terminal like a crazed halfback
headed for the goal-line with four big bags flopping like crazy. Boy, did I
nearly steamroll about three children, two old people, a poodle and a
policeman (oops)! Needless to say, I missed my flight by about 30 steps,
and on top of that, one of my bags broke open sending socks and underwear flying all over the terminal floor (how embarrassing).

As Christians we have times we carry excess baggage such as worry,
anger, envy, jealousy and bitterness while racing through the terminals of
time. They become a heavy burden and at times too much to bear. Our
knees buckle, our tempers go ballistic, and our attitude stinks, simply
because we don't allow God to carry them for us. A lot of times people
have adverse reactions like depression, violence or even suicide as a release
valve. Don't let your baggage encumber you to the point of wanting to
quit. Cast your worries and all your troubles (bags) on Him because He
cares. Believe me, bags not only slow you down, they are a down right
pain to deal with and could cause you to miss your flight to happiness.

★ ★ ★

Further Study: What bags are you carrying around with you through life?
How can God help relieve you of the heavy burdens society weighs on
you? Will you let Him today?

A TASTE TEST

Taste and see that the Lord is good.
Psalm 34:8

★ ★ ★

One of the fondest memories I have from my childhood is Thanksgiving at my grandparents' house in Norman, Oklahoma. We would load up the old station wagon with my sisters' and my bikes on the roof and head across the Red River into Sooner country. Riding on the tractor with Grandpa, feeding the cows and eating tender smoked turkey are vivid memories, but not so much as Grandma's homemade peach pies. I recall her spending hours working the crust, skinning the peaches and churning the ice cream. The phase I drooled over the most was the just-cooked pies in the window sill. Now to give you an idea of my situation, I was always about a smell away from those pies, but they were too high up in the window to reach. I remember getting a good swat (spanking) for stacking two barrels on top of each other and taking a pie (before dinner) and eating it all by myself. I might have been little, but I could eat. You better believe I knew how good they were, but my tastebuds had to taste and see for themselves to make sure.

You see, we all know that God is loving, powerful, merciful, gracious, protecting, tender, accepting, sacrificial and almighty, but do we really know? The only way to know if He really is all He says He is, is to taste of Him and experience the satisfaction. Just as I knew Grandma's pies were good, I had to make the extra effort to go to them and try 'em out. The same is true with our God. You must taste and see of God's love, mercy, faithfulness, compassion, grace and power. Take it from an expert in eating, taste and fulfillment definitely hold up to their billing.

★ ★ ★

Further Study: When did you last taste of God? How do you really taste of Him? What desires will be satisfied when you do? Taste and see for yourself today.

PROMISE REAPERS

Do not be deceived, God is not mocked; for whatever a
man sows, this he will also reap.
Galatians 6:7

★ ★ ★

What began in 1990 as the dream of Bill McCartney, former head coach of the University of Colorado Buffaloes football team, is today the fastest growing men's movement in the United States. Coach "Mac," who led his team to the national title in college football, resigned his $325,000-a-year job to practice what he preached and devote his full time and attention to his wife, kids and the Promise Keepers' movement. Prior to this radical move, his life had been a blur of off-season recruiting, late afternoon practices and weekend college road trips, with little time for his family. Coach Mac was led by his commitment to Christ to gather seventy men together for the purpose of encouragement and support in their roles as husbands and fathers. Today, supporters number in the hundreds of thousands, packing stadiums in major cities each year. This movement calls men of integrity back to their responsibility without encouraging a harsh, authoritarian leadership. Commitment to the family should not be one of control, but of research and development.

Of late, the family has been spiritually led by the woman. Our society needs to see what spiritual men, as husbands and fathers committed to Christ, look like. The Promise Keepers' movement is an attempt (it's working) to reverse this trend and encourage men to be involved at home with their time and spiritual input.

What does this movement mean to you today? Tons! You can start now to develop the qualities necessary to be a Promise Keeper. You won't just wake up transformed, or take a magic pill that turns you into a committed man of integrity and conviction. Don't think for one minute that what you are doing won't affect your tomorrow. It will! The choices and decisions you make now will in turn make you better, later. Be a man of your word; be a leader through Christ; be a man of high values; be consistent with your talk and walk. Be all you can be! You will reap what you sow. Be a Promise Keeper.

★ ★ ★

Further Study: Write down five goals you wish to attain in five years. How do you plan to attain them? When do you start pursuing?

HIDE AND SEEK

This son of mine was dead and has come to life again; he was lost,
and has now been found. And they began to be merry.
Luke 15:24

★ ★ ★

It's one game we've all played before, yet as we get older and graduate from childish games, it's still good for some fun watchin'. Ponder with
me as we descend upon a game of hide and seek with a bunch of five-year-
olds. The group selects the gullible one of the bunch to be the seeker, as
the rest scatter like flies to their secret hideouts. The seeker begins to count
to 10 (by thousands) then shouts out, "ready or not, here I come!"
Remember how you would always go to the obvious spots first and come
up empty handed, so then you would resort to phase two of the search and
rescue mission? Finally, after a few minutes, your Sherlock Holmes inves-
tigation tactics were successful. The part I never liked about this goofy
game (you too, I'll bet) was when you did such a good job of hiding that
you never got found. You were the one who wasn't told the game was
over, so you stayed in the stinky, dirty, laundry basket camouflaged in
socks, underwear and shirts with armpit stains. The object of that game is
to eventually be found, not remain concealed forever.

Everyone, and I mean everyone, you pass on the streets each day is
still, in one form or another, playing hide and seek. The sad thing is that
we all really want to be found because that means we matter. The incredible thing about God is He entered His Son (Jesus) into this game of life to
find those who are lost with no hope. No matter how macho, tough, independent, self-reliant a soul may appear to be, it's all a front. In their own
way they wiggle and make high-pitch noises and sounds to draw attention
from the seeker. As Christians, we need to listen for those noises, gestures,
comments, attitudes and outbursts which are really saying, "I'm over here.
. . come find me." The prodigal son was lost, living in a pig pen and
returned to an inaugural ball reception from his father. The same will be
true for those lost souls on earth . . . ready or not, here He comes!

★ ★ ★

Further Study: Who do you know that is lost in the game of life from Jesus?
Can you help find them?

MIND OVER MATTER

There is forgiveness with Thee.
Psalms 130:4

* * *

It's like a steel trap that snares its victims with little hope for release. Your mind and your memory can either provide freedom, or lock you in an emotional prison. Chuck Swindoll said, "Life is 10% what happens and 90% how you react to what happens." That's the key. Okay, so you don't deck someone for treating you unfairly, or practice tit-for-tat strategies either. Not so fast though! Retaliation will often take a more subtle form. The best way to ensure true forgiveness is to be aware of the sly ways people don't forgive each other, like:

Gossip–We make negative reports about someone else, driving a wedge.
Criticism (without constructive advice)–We complain and nag the people who offend us until they are as hurt as we think we are.
Withdrawal–We avoid, deprive or exclude from our plans and company those people who hurt us.
Self-appointed martyrdom–Using a real or imagined injury, we manipulate people into feeling sorry for us.
Constructive criticism–While helpful criticism encourages and corrects, even
good advice becomes "poison" when it's motivated by
disappointment and resentment.

Humility is the key to this whole forgiveness issue. Phillips Brooks wrote, "The true way to be humble is not to stoop until you are smaller than yourself, but to stand at your real height against some higher nature that will show you what the real smallness of your greatness is." Forgive and forget . . . it's the ultimate in abundant living and freedom.

* * *

Further Study: Are you a forgiving person? Do you feel that you have any bitterness towards anyone? Do you forget easily? Do you hold grudges?

PRIVILEGE NOT PROGRAM

Our Father who art in heaven hallowed be thy name.
Matthew 6:9

★ ★ ★

I wrestled over the decision to include a devotional expounding on this bit of scripture. Why? Because Christians seem to have lost their grip on the purpose of prayer designated by God. I am not a "name it, claim it" Christian (don't tune me out . . . I'm not done). Yes, yes, yes, I do believe that our God is bigger than any sickness, any financial debt, or any situation we might get ourselves into, but I don't believe we can ask God for selfish things or ones that are incompatible with scripture and expect to receive them. Take a look at how Jesus taught His disciples to pray with the Lord's Prayer. See if materialism rears its ugly head anywhere in this prayer. Instead, it teaches us to recognize God's position as God, praise His majesty, ask for daily survival tools, forgive us our mess-ups, and provide us strength to lessen our mistakes in the future.

My philosophy may appear to be that if I can't convince you, I'll confuse you, and I see by that look on your face, you're confused. Put it this way–prayer is a privilege, not a program. Prayer is an awesome moment when we enter into God's presence and communicate spiritually with Him face-to-face. Why do we let worldly thoughts enter our faith and convince us that the purpose for prayer is to gain acceptance or get our way? Don't forget that communication is not a one-way street where we talk and God listens. Part of an effective prayer life is that we "be still and know that I am God." Listen. You won't be able to hear Him in the midst of chaos. Find a Bethel (Old Testament place of worship) and be consistent in meeting your Savior on a regular basis. Make your prayer life as practical as eating and breathing . . . it's a lot more fulfilling, too! (No pun intended.)

★ ★ ★

Further Study: How often do you pray? What gets in your way of having an effective daily prayer time? Do you see prayer as a privilege? How do you pray?

HERITAGE OR INHERITANCE

Indeed, my heritage is beautiful to me.
Psalm 16:6

✶ ✶ ✶

Moses trained Joshua for leadership; Paul modeled church-planting to Timothy; Abraham exemplified sacrifice to Isaac; Noah proved obedience has its rewards to his family; Naomi mirrored care to Ruth. There are so many benefits that leaving a legacy can bring. Passing down a heritage demands character, commitment, love, staying power and a heavenly perspective. The institute called the family is God's smallest yet most productive battle formation. God's plan for parents in passing down a godly heritage or legacy requires first developing a strategy in opposition to the world's plan. scripture is packed with examples of obedient godly followers who continued the cycle through mentoring. Our world today is more concerned with trust funds and savings accounts to be passed down to ensure financial stability for their kids than a heritage of godliness. I think we could say here that "we got the cart way before the horse." Jesus modeled best for us the passing of a heritage to His twelve disciples. He was there for and with them, and left them to carry out the orders after He was gone from earth.

I realize the overwhelming reality of actually passing down character traits, beliefs and traditions, not to mention the family name. I realize that as a dad and husband your daily responsibilities are enough to drive you over the edge. I understand the war against the persistent attacks of Satan, the flesh and the world are enough to make you wanna' throw your hands up in disgust. My encouragement to you as a parent and spouse is to push through the discouraging times, which are caused in part by a lack of immediate results due to unrealistic expectations. God will honor your faithfulness (read Matthew 25:23) and your labor. Your children need a heritage far more than they need an inheritance, and the cash will run out long before the legacy. The world's plan results in a tribute to self surrounded by turmoil and division, while God's plan honors God and rests in peace and harmony. Don't give up; leave behind something of eternal value. True laborers or families can't be mass produced; they are raised up through life on life experiences.

✶ ✶ ✶

Further Study: How would you define a legacy? How does someone pass down a heritage today? What obstacle will you encounter in the process? Are you more concerned about the heritage or inheritance? Go ahead . . . hand it off.

133

THE ART OF DELEGATION

Furthermore, you shall select out of all the people able men who fear God,
men of ruth, those who hate dishonest gain, and you shall delegate
to them and place them as leaders over thousands, hundreds,
fifties and tens. So it will be easier for you, and they
will bear the burden with you. If you do these
things and God so commands you, then
you will be able to endure.
Exodus 18:21-23

★ ★ ★

Working with people, which all of us are doing or will be doing, is a fun task. One lost art that I see missing from the centerpiece of the godly living room is delegation. Webster's defines delegation as "to commit or entrust authority to another person as an agent." We have far too many people who need to do it all, all the time. The word "training" (teaching) comes to mind here for the simple reason that those folks who have the philosophy "if you want something done right, do it yourself" seem to have lost sight. Granted, you want your trainee (pupil) to fall on his/her face, but not lose face in a project. You see, Jesus used another word for training and that is discipleship.

In this passage, Moses takes a little advice from his father-in-law. Moses is to answer all questions, meet everyone's needs and play referee too? Not alone, he's not. This is the scene where the pop-in-law flies onto the set and sheds a little wisdom of prior knowledge to the formula of leadership/delegation (they go hand-in-hand, you know). The formula for successful delegation of a project, or task, is to find folks who possess the character qualities listed in scripture, create the vision for them, then ask the "delegate-to-be" to tell you what you told him before setting out on this voyage. First, make sure you don't set someone up for failure by delegating to him a task that you know he doesn't have the skills to pull off. You must know your people, as Jesus did. Second, the proper steps to training are as follows: number one, model how you want it done; number two, do it with the trainee; and number three, leave and let them do it alone. It's as simple as one, two, three. Try it!

★ ★ ★

Further Study: What was the last thing you delegated? Did they qualify with the formula?

134

MOM

Her children arise up and call her blessed, her husband also, and he prizes her.
Proverbs 31:28

Her ability to love is exceeded only by God's love itself.
Rex Burns

All that I am or hope to be, I owe to my angel mother.
Abraham Lincoln

It's at our mother's knee that we acquire our noblest and truest and highest ideals. Mark Twain

★ ★ ★

The love of a mother is never exhausted; it never changes, and it never tires. Our society has placed a demeaning connotation on the title of housewife and mom. What people tend to forget is that it's a mother who makes a house a home. Career seems to have edged out the most important job on this earth, mothering a child. I need a little room on this page to flat out brag on my wife, who is the greatest mother to my three boys. My sons worship the precious ground she walks on. Why? Because she cares like God cares for them. No, she's not perfect by any means, but you'll have a heck of a time convincing my boys she's not. When God created the female, He personally installed in their chassis a gift for nurturing that seems to work on auto-pilot all day, every day. There is no greater responsibility or job, yesterday, today or in our hi-tech future, that equals motherhood. I try (as a father), but I can't hold a candle to my wife when it comes to raising God-fearing children. She soothes with her voice and she loves with her heart.

No matter what you might think of your mom, realize this–she's the only mom you'll ever have. Respect your mom, honor your mom, care for your mom, protect your mom, pray for your mom, encourage your mom, and   lastly . . . value her.

★ ★ ★

Further Study: Go right now, no matter where she is and tell your mom you love her. Write her a love note, give her a hug, serve her, make her breakfast in bed, do your chores without being told. Tonight, hit your knees and pray for your mom and the mom you want to be or marry.

CATCH THE VISION

Where there is no vision the people perish.
Proverbs 29:18

★ ★ ★

Years ago before Disney grew into the number one tourist attraction in North America, Walt Disney created a vision. During the building and before the completion of Disneyland in California, he put together a huge banquet/cookout which cost three million dollars for all the workers who would be involved in building this theme park. The plumbers, concrete layers, electricians, roofers, welders, painters, bull-dozer operators, survey-ors, crane operators, and so on, were all gonna' be invited to this bash. Walt Disney had the architects design a small "model" of the finished prod-uct, so that all these workers would be able to see it during the banquet. The purpose was to create a vision in the eyes of each worker so they just didn't hammer a nail, wire a building, weld some pipe, lay some concrete, survey the dirt, paint a building or bull-doze a rock. After seeing the model, the workers wouldn't just put forth their muscle and effort, but also put their hearts into their work.

We, too, need to have a vision for all that we do in this life. We need to catch a dream of not just what we're doing but who we're doing it for and its purpose. You've got to have a vision for being a follower of Jesus, or your gas tank will run dry quickly. You've got to see the reason for wait-ing until marriage to have sex. You must see that there is a purpose for spending time in God's Word and praying to Him. See the light at the end of the tunnel today, and your path will be a lot easier to follow because of focusing on it. Believe you me, I think Disneyland is the neatest spot on earth, but it can't hold a candle to your spot in heaven. It won't cost you a three million dollar banquet to catch this vision, just a little time spent in the Word. And who knows, maybe Mickey and Minnie will be waiting at those pearly gates greeting you on the way in.

★ ★ ★

Further Study: Do you have a vision? Of what? How can a spiritual vision help you in your walk with Christ? How can it help you remain pure? Where can you catch this vision?

NOSE TO NOSE

Faithful are the wounds of a friend, but deceitful are the kisses of an enemy.
Psalms 27:6

☆ ☆ ☆

Why doesn't everyone think like you? Why did God have to create so many, so differently? As the gray hair begins to sprout on your head like daisies in a field, you'll realize how difficult it is to get along well with people. Whether at work, on a team, in a club, or even in the midst of your own family, you'll always find conflicts in interests and beliefs. The problem rears its ugly head when we don't handle differences as God intended. Violence and anger seem to be popular means of dealing with differences. Why? Because we don't realize that difference can be the sharp tool God uses to chip away character flaws. Think about it, confrontation has a way of bringing out both the best and the worst in us.

Our society seems to have lost the meaning of friendship. We label as friends those who are really only acquaintances. A real friend is someone for whom you would lay down your life. A friend is someone who sticks closer than a blood relative through the highs and lows. A friend loves enough to point out flaws in our character in order to make us better. A friend warns us of upcoming dangers and hazards we may soon encounter. A friend loves at all times. Don't be afraid to point out, not judge, a friend's weaknesses that are inhibiting a fulfilling life with Christ. Don't nit-pick issues that don't matter, choose what mountains to climb with a friend and go for it. Deal with issues that go against scripture. To love a friend, you'll have to learn to be one first!

☆ ☆ ☆

Further Study: What is your definition of friendship? Are you a real friend? What could make you a better friend? Ask a friend what you could do to be a better friend.

EXPRESSING INDIVIDUALITY

I will give thanks to thee, for I am fearfully and wonderfully made;
wonderful are thy works, and my soul knows it very well.
Psalms 139:14

★ ★ ★

When in doubt, blame it on a low self-image, right? It seems like everybody who is anybody wants a scapegoat, so we have chosen the old self-worth. The problem with not only non-believers, but Christians too, is that we don't see like God sees. A friend of mine, a very talented Christian singer, Billy Sprague, sings a song with catchy lyrics that say, "I am as I am if I am all I see, but if He is all I see, then I see me as He" (confusing, isn't it?). The gist of it simply states that when we put our focus on the Creator and not the creation (me), then the fog of worthlessness is lifted.

Get this . . . you need to be taking a victory lap, not singin' the blues about you as a valuable vessel. You need to be spending less time trying to revamp the system and more time sharpening up what and who you are. Listen to me for one minute, and I promise you I won't stutter and make sure your ears don't flap, but you are wonderfully made! Okay, was that loud enough for ya'? Let me clue your brain in to this wave, too . . . God doesn't make junk! Hear that too? We all, including myself, should jump out of bed like a missile off the launch pad, throw our hands up heavenward and say, "thanks a ton, God, for making me like me." What a new outlook on life, not having to be something you're not. If you're created to be a duck then don't try to be like your neighboring squirrels (ducks look stupid climbing trees and squirrels look even dumber swimming). Before you go to bed tonight I want you to read the verse above 10 times and try to memorize it (oh no, homework, dude!), cuz' it's worth your time.

★ ★ ★

Further Study: Do you know deep in your soul that you are a wonderful creation? Do you feel like a castle or a shack? According to this verse, what did God create? Do you believe it?

OUT OF BOUNDS

Now the deeds of the flesh are evident, which are: immorality, impurity, sensuality, idolatry, sorcery, enmities, strife, jealousy, outburst of anger, disputes, dissentions, factions, envying, drunkenness, carousing, and things like these, of which I forewarn you just as I have forewarned you that those who practice such things shall not inherit the Kingdom of God.
Galatians 5:19-21

★ ★ ★

Close your eyes for a moment and imagine a football game with no end zone, a basketball game with no hoop, a golf course with no fairway, a tennis match with no net, and a track or swim meet with no lanes. Now, correct me if I'm wrong, but that would be the ultimate in confusion. Basketball without sidelines, referees or a goal is rugby. If you have ever been on a canoe or raft trip down a long river in Colorado you know the ride is defined by the beauty of cliffs that grow out of the river banks up to the clouds. Boundaries communicate a standard set by a scholar of the game and help produce a sport that's fun, yet fair to all.

Whether you like them or not, agree or disagree, you live in a civilization that has a few rules and boundaries. They are in place to help, not hurt you. Why a speed limit? So you don't kill yourself or others. Why gun laws? So no one shoots you. Why a judicial system? So everyone goes by the same laws. God has set in place rules and laws that are there for your benefit. The Ten Commandments are not a list of suggestions. Do yourself a favor and stay in the bounds that God laid down. It makes life so much easier and less painful. God is not some cosmic kill-joy looking to punish you for living. He desires to provide a wonderful, fulfilling, joyful game of life . . . just stay in bounds or you'll lose.

★ ★ ★

Further Study: Why are there rules? Why do sports have boundaries—to help the game or destroy it? Do you play in or out of bounds in God's game most of the time? What can you do to stay in bounds more often?

GRATITUDE

Let the peace of Christ rule in your hearts, to which indeed you
were called in one body, and be thankful.
Colossians 3:15

✷ ✷ ✷

Mother Theresa, one of the most godly women to roam this planet, told this story in an address to the National Prayer Breakfast. In a foreign country one evening, she went out and picked up four people from off the streets (bums). One of the four was in sad shape, so she told the other three, "I will take care of the one in the worst condition." Mother Theresa did for her all that her love could do. She put her in a warm bed, and there was a smile on her face as she did so. The sick woman took her hand and said only two words, "Thank you," and then she died. Mother Teresa addressed the group, "I couldn't help but examine my conscience before her. I asked myself what would I say if I were in her place? My answer was simple. I would have said I'm hungry, dying and in pain. She gave me much more than I gave her (a bed), she gave me her grateful love and died with a smile on her face."

Isn't it ironic that gratitude brings a smile to people and becomes such a wonderful gift? Mother Theresa had such a neat perspective and wonderful outlook on life. God puts you in situations daily where you can take the honors or give the glory to Him—your choice. To be grateful means to appreciate the kindness and grace you have been given or shown. Calvary (the cross) is a supreme (and we're not talking pizza) example of gratitude. Be thankful for every day you live and all the many blessings which come standard with each day.

✷ ✷ ✷

Further Study: For what or whom are you thankful? What does gratitude mean to you? Are you one of those who takes things for granted? Why? How can you be grateful for all you have? Will you? When? How?

COSMETIC CHAOS

For God sees not as man sees, for man looks at the outward
appearance, but the Lord looks at the heart.
1 Samuel 16:7

★ ★ ★

Thank God we live by the laws of the Creator and not the created! It seems like we live in a world of public displays, or like fish in a fish bowl where everything and everyone is judged on appearance. This cosmetic cosmos we call earth seems to have lost its perspective on what really matters and what doesn't. I heard a story of a unique burglary which took place in the windy city of Chicago, but the robbers didn't steal anything. They broke into a department store and switched price tags to make cheap items expensive and expensive merchandise cheap. A few hours past the store's opening, one chilly Monday morning, the salespeople began to notice something was definitely amiss. It seems that Satan (the thief) has come into our store (life) and switched around our priorities. He has taken the superficial and made it more important than the inward qualities of the heart. Can you imagine marrying someone for his/her appearance only, knowing full well that everyone gets older, grayer, more wrinkled and less mobile by the day? Our hearts, however, (Jesus' temple) get better by the day and more attractive by the hour. How refreshing it would be to have someone walk up and say, "you have a beautiful heart," or "your heart gets better lookin' everyday!"

It never fails that God's way is the right way. What a difference it would make in our social system if we would see as God sees.

★ ★ ★

Further Study: How do you feel today about yourself? Are you looking from God's eyes?

A FRIEND IN DEED

A man (or woman) *of many friends comes to ruin, but there is
a friend who sticks closer than any brother.*
Proverbs 18:24

★ ★ ★

You can't live with 'em, and you can't live without 'em. If there is one area considered as important as tick spray is to a dog, it's friendships. Every person alive today (including you) desires close, intimate relationships with others outside of dating. The one thing all these high-powered psychologists and psychiatrists, both secular and Christian, agree upon is that everyone has two needs. One is the need to be loved; the second is the need to love someone else. You know our dating relationships would be a lot longer lasting and closer if they started out as a friendship first and then graduated into a dating relationship. Marriages would be easier and more fruitful if they were an extended friendship which blossomed into a lifelong commitment.

Growing up, I didn't come from a church-going, meal praying family. I attribute my spiritual guidance to my uncompromising Christian friends. The Bible says, "bad company (not the rock group either) corrupts good morals." How often we run around with whom we may call friends, but who are only mere acquaintances, in actuality. If we use God's definition of true friendship to pick our friends, I think we would not be as apt to say, "I have tons of friends." A real friend is one who is like-minded with you in beliefs, ethics, morals and standards, one who challenges you to grow closer with Christ before growing closer to him, one who will stick with you through the highs and lows, ins and outs.

God gives you the model relationship and then leaves it up to you to follow the instruction manual (Bible) and build it. Don't hang out with the pigs if you don't want to end up in the mud. If you have a friend (not acquaintance) who sticks with you like a fly to fly paper, then invest your heart in him/her. Use your tongue wisely and be as loyal as a dog is to his owner. Believe me, this will be one investment with big returns even when the market falls.

★ ★ ★

Further Study: Who would you die for out of your friends today? Why or why not? Are the reasons derived from scripture?

BATH TIME

*If we confess our sins, He is faithful and just to forgive us our sin
and cleanse us from all unrighteousness.*
1 John 1:9

★ ★ ★

There is no time more fun at my household than a home cooked supper, followed up with the priceless dessert of "bath time." The kids can hardly finish their last bite before they are dashing off up the stairs, leaving a trail of clothes, headed for that big warm bath filled with Mr. Bubble. I always thought (that is, until I had kids) that the sole goal for a bath was to get clean. The purpose, to my surprise, of baths is to experiment with toys to see which float and which don't, how long it takes little brother to start kicking after holding him under for a new record or what amount of water can be deposited on the floor before Dad gets mad. No matter how you've grown up, you'll probably always remember those tub-times, and if not, you will when the kiddos come.

So often in scripture you'll find a passage, word, or verse that you have heard so much that you become numb to it. This passage is one of those that you just glide right past as you fly through your quiet time. Do you see two mighty characteristics of God . . . faithful and just? Did you miss the part about what you have to do in order for Him to respond? How about . . . you confess your mistakes; He cleanses you. In John 13:10 Jesus explains to Peter, prior to the last supper and after He had washed Peter's feet, that there was not a need to take another bath (accept Christ as your Savior again). Just repent daily (wash your feet) to be cleansed and make things right with God. Wow, what a deal! How easy it is if we just stay soft at heart, He gives us our own "bath time" cleansing.

★ ★ ★

Further Study: How often do you have a "bath time" with God? Do you need a bath today?

TURN OR BURN

Suffer hardship with me, as a good soldier of Christ Jesus.
2 Timothy 2:3

★ ★ ★

In July of 64 AD, a fire broke out in a ghetto area of Rome and burned down half the city. The rumor was that Nero did it to free up space for new building plans, but his scapegoat became the Christians in Rome and an active pursuit to persecute Christians began. Paul was in prison, but a guy named Demas wasn't, and he decided to run before he was persecuted and condemned as well. He decided to run to his home in Thessalonica (2 Timothy 4:10). His concern for safety in this present world caused him to lose sight of the future kingdom which Paul so eagerly awaited.

When Paul referred to being in love with this world, he was speaking of its prosperity, profit and fame. To Demas, life was too precious and short, too full of delight, to be thrown into Nero's lions' den as an amusement for thousands of bloodthirsty spectators. He recalled all the friends and fortune he left behind to become a Christian, and his excitement for missionary work with Paul faded. Demas had not heeded Paul's advice to set his "affection on things above, not on things on this earth" (Colossians 3:2), and he had slowly become more and more "conformed to the world" (Romans 12:2). As a result of this, Demas was unwilling to maintain his commitment to Paul and God during that time of intense pressure and persecution.

The true test of ourselves and our allegiance is when the heat is turned up. You really don't know what level of commitment you or the other party has in a friendship, working relationship, marriage or to God until everything ain't goin' so good and you "bail out." Are you one who jumps ship when your life begins to take on water (hard times), or are you one who sucks it up and goes down with the ship? The true test of commitment is when faith is all you have, but it's all you need. The true test of a race isn't how you start, but if you finish.

★ ★ ★

Further Study: Define commitment in your terms, then in God's terms. How committed are you when the walls fall down around you and things look bleak? How can you prepare now for those tough times?

144

Now You See It, Now You Don't

You do not know what tomorrow has in store . . . your life is but a vapor.
James 4:14

★ ★ ★

It would have been considered a normal day at the office. At 9:03 a.m. on April 19, 1995, federal employees were doing what needed doing in downtown Oklahoma City at the Alfred P. Murrah Federal Building. At 9:04 a.m. the blast from a 24-foot rental truck filled with explosives sent a shock wave, causing total destruction at the site and severe damage to buildings blocks away. Hundreds of fatalities and injuries resulted from the blast consisting of two tons of ammonium nitrate fertilizer, doused in fuel oil, ignited by some sort of detonator. This terrorist act was the worst in U.S. history and stunned the American public. Who and why? Timothy James McVeigh, a 27 year old man portrayed by some in the media as easygoing and introspective, certainly did not seem to fit the profile of someone who could cause this terror. Since returning from the Gulf War, though, he reportedly fathered an illegitimate child, lost jobs, drank a lot, fought often, set off explosives, bought guns, occasionally attended rightwing militia group meetings, and lived like a nomad. Timothy was angry at the world (especially the government) for the way the cult compound in Waco, Texas, was handled. He harbored vengeance, fueled by an anger without regard for life, just as long as his statement was made.

Four days after this morning of terror, I was in Oklahoma City for a speaking engagement. I rented a car and was compelled to drive downtown to see the devastation. I stood by the roped off building, wept and prayed for the victims and their families. I thought about the one minute (9:03) prior to the blast and one minute after (9:05). One minute alive . . . the next dead. I recalled the verse in James that illustrated to me that our life is a mist . . . the wisp of steam that rises off an early morning cup of coffee, then vanishes. Life is short and unpredictable. My prayer was that they all (children, men, and women) went to heaven . . . Amen.

★ ★ ★

Further Study: What is anger? How is it manifested? How do you control it? What happens if it's not dealt with?

GIFTED

I will give thanks to Thee, for I am fearfully and wonderfully made;
wonderful are Thy works, and my soul knows it well.
Psalms 139:14

★ ★ ★

There is nothing quite like laying on your back, gazing up on a crystal clear night, looking at the stars. On a dark, quiet night sitting alone just looking up in the sky, at first glance, all the stars seem to be identical. But if you look through a telescope you will notice differences in size, color, intensity, shape and structure. I bet if you were to crack a few of those stars open like an egg, you'd find each one is even composed differently. You can say the same of people. How similar one seems to the other, just like stars, until you look more closely and get to know them. At that point, a special transformation of thinking and perspective occurs, and you realize we all are uniquely different. Even a person's own name is a unique characteristic. You soon realize that each person is made up of a variety of hopes, dreams, theories, perspectives, goals and cherished thoughts. It's the unique differences that allow us to exist separately and yet combine harmoniously like the multiple pieces of a jigsaw puzzle fit together to form a whole.

God has specifically made each of us different, but at the same time He gave us equal opportunity to develop our gifts and talents. Utilize your special God-given gifts as only you can and learn to accept and encourage the talents of others. Throw away petty jealousy and have the mature attitude that encourages others to be all they were meant to be in Christ. If you can't win the race yourself, make sure the guy that beats you breaks the world record. Be a Barnabus who saw his limits, but saw Paul's exceptional gifts and encouraged him to use them. Plant trees that you'll never sit under . . . that's a Christian outlook.

★ ★ ★

Further Study: List what you think your talents are. Now, how do you utilize these gifts for God? Are you one of those who doesn't see his/her talents, just those of others? Take a minute to ask God to use you and your talents toda

IDENTITY CRISIS

To the degree that you share in the sufferings of Christ, keep on rejoicing.
1 Peter 4:13

✯ ✯ ✯

In the town of Stepanvan, Armenia, there lives a woman that everyone calls "Palasan's wife." She has her own name, of course, but the people of this small town call her by her husband's name to show her honor. In 1988, a devastating earthquake struck this town in the early noon hour. Mr. Palasan was at work when the quake hit, and he rushed over to the elementary school his son attended. By the time he arrived, the school was already destroyed, but he entered the building to carry children outside to safety. He saved 28 children, but when he went back inside for a final check, an aftershock hit. The school building completely collapsed, and Mr. Palasan was killed.

Being the son of a professional football player was a great honor. To be associated with him when I went to the University of Oklahoma and played basketball (even though his illustrious career there was in football) was also a great honor. Sometimes a person's greatest honor is not who they are but to whom they are related. The highest honor of any believer is to be called a disciple of Jesus Christ, who laid down His life for all people. To be called "child of God" is more of an identity and honor than any other name in the universe. The Armenian woman was honored to be called "Palasan's wife." It is much more of an honor to be called "a disciple of Christ."

✯ ✯ ✯

Further Study: Who do people say that you are? Are you associated with Christ? Do people see you in your lifestyle as a relative of the Creator? Why or why not? How can you obtain that title? Are you willing to do what it takes to get it?

THE MAJORITY

Blessed is the man who doesn't walk in the counsel of the wicked,
stand in the way of sinners or sit in the seat of mockers.
Psalm 1:1

★ ★ ★

You live in a civilization where the majority has ruled throughout history. The greatest injustices of history have been unchecked "majority rule." It was the majority that crucified Christ, burned Christians at the stake, established slavery in the South, chuckled when Columbus said the world was round, cut off the ears of John Pym because he advocated the liberty of the press, put Hitler into power and overturned Roe v. Wade to legalize abortion. As you can see (and I'm sure you could add a lot more to this list), the majority is not necessarily always best for you or your country.

As a Christian you have the governing authority to choose what is right or wrong, to decide to run with the majority and to not run with the minority. People in our culture (including Christians) have a natural tendency to always choose the easy way. The problem comes when the easy way isn't the right way. You didn't see Jesus choosing the easy way, did you? You didn't hear Him saying, "Hey, these spikes in my wrists and this thorn crown on my head are a pain, so I quit." Jesus, the ultimate role model, shows and proves that most of the time the harder way (less traveled) is the best way. Every day you face the intersection of choosing to go with the flow or swim against the current (like a salmon). It's usually the majority that will be drinking, getting divorced, cheating on tests, not telling the truth or trying pre-marital sex. I'm definitely not telling you choosing the harder way will be easy, but neither did Jesus. You'll have to have the faith, which is what it takes to stand your ground and do what Jesus would do in every situation and circumstance. Most of the time it's what the few do that leave a lasting impact on the world for Christ.

★ ★ ★

Further Study: Why do most vote with the majority? How tough is it for you to go against the flow? Will you do it today? Why or why not? What kind of impact will you have for standing firm in your faith?

HOPE SET HIGH

And hope does not disappoint us because God has poured out his love into our hearts by the Holy Spirit, whom he has given us.
Romans 5:5

★ ★ ★

Now, here is a classic. Do you remember the childhood movie about the circus elephant with the enormous ears? How at first he was mocked and abused by some (the crows), and then, he was praised and applauded by all (the crowd)? *Dumbo* is a classic because it shows how an apparent goof can become a gift. The circus mouse plays a key role in the movie as the one who initiates the forward progress. He has a desire for Dumbo with expectations of success. He looks past the obvious to see the hope. Realize that hope will never disappoint you. How does the mouse pull this off? What else . . . the magic feather. Remember that it was Dumbo's belief in the feather which allowed him to soar through the air with the greatest of ease.

You and I have a responsibility to be like the mouse and desire others to be better than ourselves. Set goals to serve the servants; delegate yourself out of a job; be a "give fanatic" (anything to anyone). Give what you're asking . . . magic feathers, of course. That little something extra which will encourage someone else to succeed (maybe before you do). It's not the final destination that is so exciting; it's the journey. It's not the final bang but every step along the way. Give out feathers on the journey and not at the finish line. You realize that to do this you'll need the mind set of Christ (think like Him). Jesus succeeded because He had hope in heaven with His Father. When the world tells you to put all your hope in money, clothes, cars, medicine, houses, jobs, etc., you'll have to fight the thought and focus on the truth. Our hope in Christ is the promise of tomorrow. Dumbo may have started out his career as the brunt of jokes, but he ended up the talk of the town with a little help from a hope giver (the mouse) with a magic wand (the feather).

★ ★ ★

Further Study: What is a magic feather to you? What magic feather can you give to someone else today?

Discharged

*In this you greatly rejoice, though now for a little while you may
have had to suffer grief in all kinds of trials.*
1 Peter 1:6

★ ★ ★

I'm slowly figuring out this family stuff. I'll do my best to try and
share a few helpful hints so that your learning curve will be less dramatic.
First and foremost, when you find out you're "expecting," purchase a video
camcorder. There are about 2,000 different types of camcorders on the
market, old fashioned, big ones, palm size or picture view. Costs range
from hundreds to thousands, depending on your weakness for gimmicks
(bells and whistles), or your preference for quality. You can buy all sorts of
junk with them like bags, tripods and lenses. Whatever you buy, you'd best
get several batteries and lots of video tape.

After I purchased my camcorder, I then read the instructions (which
is uncommon for me) on the use of the battery. The manufacturer recom-
mend that the battery should completely discharge before recharging it,
especially the first few times. This procedure actually increases the
endurance of the battery.

In a like manner, our trials in life "discharge" us, emptying our dependence on self (our own human strength) and increasing our capacity to
receive God's limitless power to endure. It's not easy to totally eliminate
self and allow God to intervene as our true power source. To "discharge"
means to acknowledge that we are incapable, yet our Savior is very capable. Trials are in our path to teach us endurance, to mature us, and to deep-
en our faith and love for God. Next time you're playing with one of those
one-eyed monsters and the battery runs out, recall that the same will happen to you someday. Recharge it to full power . . . Jesus will recharge you.

★ ★ ★

Further Study: How do you handle the times when you are completely
depleted of self? How do you recharge yourself? Is God anywhere in the
picture? Why does God allow trials to discharge you?

CROSS EXAMINATION

You who are going to destroy the temple and rebuild it in three days, save Yourself! If you are the Son of God, come down off that cross.
Matthew 27:40

☆ ☆ ☆

If you've never seen it on TV, you surely have seen this rush hour of rhetoric take place on the evening news. It's a dueling tongue tango between two attorneys (that's a tongue twister if I've ever seen one) which takes place daily across this country. The arena is a big courtroom, the referee is the judge (the dude in the black robe with a mallet), the coaches are the lawyers (dressed in starch), the player is the accused (scared spitless), and the onlookers are the jurors (the ones summoned to do this). The prosecutor and the defender are going at it, like two cats after the same mouse, politicizing to win the votes of the jurors. They call on witnesses and testimonies of folks and begin to cross-examine them to shreds. What takes place during a cross examination is that a witness is called to the stand by the opposing party for the purpose of testing the reliability of his previous testimony. Boy howdy, that's when all the prior law school know-how comes in to play and things get ugly.

Read the verse above again . . . I'll wait for ya'. Okay, did you see it or even hear it from the mouthy mockers? They were cross examining Jesus right there. Those worthless chumps were checking out the reliability of Jesus' previous statement. The problem is that they didn't or couldn't see the tree cuz' of the forest. What they should have been doing instead of a cross examination is an examination of the cross . . . get it? They didn't see what was happening right in front of their flappin' lips. They didn't realize the most important trial in history had taken place, and the jury found Jesus guilty of nothing but fulfilling prophecy. I would have to say that the scene in this courtroom was not, and never will be, re-enacted in any court of law again. Gahl-Lee, aren't you glad Jesus didn't decide to come down off that cross and commence kickin' some tail? That was what I'd have done, but then again that's exactly why I'm not the Savior and Jesus is. He can handle the toughest cross examination to this day.

☆ ☆ ☆

Further Study: Do you daily cross examine God or examine the cross? Why not? How can you begin today? Will you? Who will hold you accountable to do that?

151

Resolving Conflict

Be angry yet do not sin; do not let the sun go down on your anger.
Ephesians 4:26

★ ★ ★

You know what? The older you become, the more you're gonna' realize how different and unique people really are. If you're lucky, you'll realize just how unusual people think, act, believe, walk and talk. In your search, you may also arrive at the brilliant conclusion that along with differences, conflict also seems to arise. And where conflict lives, you'll find strife as its neighbor. Strife resides next door to disharmony and anger. Now, after that boring little speech, I'd like to walk you through a way to solve the problem of anger and bitterness with a set of guidelines. These can be called "The Twelve Ground Rules of Confrontation by Communication."

Acknowledge your contribution to the problem.
Stick to today's problem and don't use the past as ammo (no "you always" or "you never" phrases).
Identify the real issue at hand; don't deal with the layers surrounding it.
Express your feelings and emotion with statements that begin with "I" instead of "you."
Avoid analyzing the other person's character (talk or behavior).
Avoid counterattacks and accept criticism graciously as a mature person.
Avoid "mind reading" what the other person means by a comment.
Keep short accounts (don't let the sun go down on your anger).
Maintain control of your tongue and emotions.
Don't attempt to win; seek mutually satisfying solutions to your disagreements.
No hitting below the belt (no cut-downs allowed).
When any of the above rules are broken, call a foul and get back on track.

If a problem should arise between you and anyone else, you must "get it right" with them soon. Remember, you don't make things right or resolve conflicts through gossip, letters, or denial–you do it by face-to-face communication. Good luck!

★ ★ ★

Further Study: Who do you have anger toward today? When are you gonna' resolve it? Today?

MARATHON RUNNERS

Now faith is the assurance of things hoped for and
the conviction of things not yet seen.
Hebrews 11:1

★ ★ ★

Have you ever asked yourself why this race we call Christianity is a marathon and not a sprint? Boy, oh boy, would it be one heck of a lot less tiring and complicated if it was. Just think . . . if it was a sprint, it would be like a fast food drive-through where we put our order in and in just a matter of seconds could see the end product. Take a look at some people of the past whom God called to strap on the lightweight running shoes and start runnin'. Noah, for instance, was called to build a yacht in the middle of a dry spell in preparation for one whopper of a downpour that would last 40 days. One hundred and twenty years after God commanded those crazy antics it happened . . . and boy did it happen! For Noah's willingness to run, God spared his life and his family's. Look at Sarah, Abraham's wife who was unable to have kids, and then at the age of 90 became pregnant with Isaac. Imagine what the neighbors said! What about Moses who was called to lead some three million whiny babies out of slavery and pulled off a few smooth moves along the way like parting a sea, making a river turn to blood and watching his cane become an irate snake?

The reason we are called to this marathon is because we don't need faith or training to run a sprint. We can see the finish in a sprint from the start but we can't in a marathon. Anyone can run a sprint any time (it may take a calendar year) and finish, but a marathon takes extensive training and sacrifice. Admit it, we need God's help to finish this long race with the faith that He will have a final finishing place (heaven) to rest. Our reward is eternal, our endurance imperative, and our course unpredictable, yet exciting. So what are you waiting for . . . on your mark, get set, go!

★ ★ ★

Further Study: What is the toughest part of your race? What causes you to want to quit? How can others before you like Noah, Sarah, and Moses inspire you today?

153

SHOCK ADS

*Jesus replied, "Love the Lord your God with all your heart
and with all your soul and with all your mind."*
Matthew 22:37

★ ★ ★

"Whatever it takes to get their attention," is the motto of the ad
agencies. The competition is getting so fierce, so dog-eat-dog, that they
will try just about any shock method to stimulate the viewer to purchase.
The Independent Media Network based in London, England, was the first
to set the perverted pace as they allowed new shock ads to be aired on TV.
They showed horse corpses falling two stories, transvestites in cabs, top-
less women, bondage, mock sex, and to top it off, dismembered body parts.
The point is that the folks who are supposed to be screening these ads
have instead bought into the hype. Now, you might be saying, "Hey, that's
in London, not Dallas," but I'm saying it's on its way to good ol' America
in just a matter of time.

Our human (sinful) nature is and always will be on the fast track to
hell if we let it take its natural course. The TV is gonna' get worse, the
domestic violence, the chemical abuse, killing of babies, homosexual activity,   disease . . . need I go on? Jesus is the one and only answer to our
problems. Whether here or abroad, via media or on the streets, in the clinics or in the hospitals. Our love (passion) must be for God Almighty and
not for the newest style or latest car. Our love must first be for God, above
the opposite sex, career placement or dollar bills. Come on, "Holmes," how
tough is it to see that without Him we crater and with Him we climb? This
devotion, I'm sure, is not a revelation in Calvinistic Theology, but it is an
attempt to get you off your content behinds and on your faithful knees.
Loving God is not a one time decision that lasts forever . . . it should be
renewed daily.

★ ★ ★

Further Study: Do you really love God? How much? When? For how long?
Daily? Weekly? Monthly? How about lifely (is that a word)?

BELIEVE YOU . . . ME

*Glory to God in the highest, and on earth, peace among men
with whom I am well pleased.*
Luke 2:14

★ ★ ★

One of the greatest storylines ever placed in a film can be found in the movie *Hook*. Robin Williams played a "success-driven" father who desired to love his family, but was caught up in the corporate scene. His children ran away to the fantasy world of "Neverland" to look for happiness, but ran into "Captain Hook" (played by Dustin Hoffman). The children's father became Peter Pan in search of his kidnapped kids, along with his trusty side-kick, "Tinker Bell," played by none other than Julia Roberts. Pete and Tinker teamed up with a ruddy band of young brigades to bring down "Hook" and his not-so-merry men. In the climax, Peter Pan and Captain Hook faced each other in a final duel of swords. At one point during the fight, it looked as if Hook would be victorious. Peter seemed without hope, until . . . his grungie brigade of boys quietly began to chant, "I believe in you . . . Peter, I believe in you." This gave Peter a sudden burst of energy and new-found confidence to ultimately defeat Hook, return to reality, and become a great dad.

I enjoyed this movie most, not because of the Academy Award acting or special effects, but for the one punch line, "I believe in you." What an awesome transformation occurs when we're told that someone out there believes in us. God said of Jesus, "This is my Son with whom I am well pleased." The flip side of this statement shows how to believe in someone else (verbally). There is no mountain you can't climb or tough time you can't overcome knowing that someone believes in you. Being believed in is just one step beneath being told you're loved. In fact, they should go together like peas and carrots (a Forrest Gump line). Show your confidence, support, and trust, in someone today by telling them you believe in them . . . start with your Savior first.

★ ★ ★

Further Study: Who was the last person you told, "I believe in you?" Who has said they believe in you? Does God believe in you? How do you know? Go tell someone!

URGED TO MERGE

This is the will of God, your sanctification; that is,
that you abstain from sexual immorality.
1 Thessalonians 4:3

★ ★ ★

By the time a young person finishes high school, he/she will have spent 18,000 hours in front of the boob-tube (TV) and only 12,000 hours in class. That is equal to more than two years spent staring at a hi-tech fish bowl. Daytime television contains 50 percent more sexual references than "prime time," so you can see why it's so popular. Sixty percent of graduating teenagers say they learned about the "birds and bees" not from their parents or sex education class, but via the television. Take a second and read through some facts that may just enlighten you about the urging from our society to have sex before marriage:

The average American teenager has had sex before their 16th birthday.
57% of high school and 79% of college students polled say they have lost their virginity.
80% of all teenage intercourse is spontaneous, not planned.
Reasons for having premarital sex are 1) peer pressure, 2) everyone's doing it, 3) curiosity, 4) gratification–not for love.
39% of high school and 58% of college students use contraceptives when having sex.
More people have died of AIDS than died in Vietnam.
(Statistics accumulated from USA Today, Journal of Marriage & Family, Center for Disease Control, Planned Parenthood)

Our sick society has discovered that exploiting young people for money is big business. We use sex to sell cigarettes, cars, toys, sports and movies. You can't read, see or hear anything today without catching a sexual reference. You, yes you, must decide where you stand and what you're standing for. Sex is not some sneaky, ugly, evil, ritualistic act portrayed by Hollywood, but a function designed specifically by God. What our Creator planned, the world has perverted. Resist the urge to merge and willfully wait until marriage . . . it is well worth it.

★ ★ ★

Further Study: Why wait? Give reasons to wait. Why does God want us to wait until marriage? What steps can keep you out of a bad situation? Are you willing to wait?

WARNING LABELS

*By faith Noah, when being warned about things not yet seen, in holy fear
built an ark to save his family. By his faith he condemned the world
and became heir of the righteousness that comes by faith.*
Hebrews 11:7

★ ★ ★

You see them everywhere if you look closely. They inform, encourage and instruct concerning possible dangers. What are they? Warning labels. You've seen them on medicines, chemicals, sports equipment, electric devices and on heavy machinery. Their purpose is like the ol' saying goes, "an ounce of prevention is worth a pound of cure." If you defy them, you could be harmed or possibly, even killed. If you play with fire, you will probably get burned . . . if you don't heed the warning, you'll probably feel the effects. Why is it that our old self steps in and whispers lies to us like, "Go ahead, it couldn't be that bad," or, "Step out, take a chance, live life to its fullest."

God's word is full of thousands of warning labels to communicate the dangers ahead and describe the hazards that could occur if overlooked. Isn't it great that we have a Master who looks out for us more than we do? What an awesome way of showing one's love for another! How incredible it is to tell others of potential potholes on life's highways and byways. The real question is do you listen and obey them? Do you actually take the warnings from your navigator (God) that bad weather could be ahead if you continue flying as you are? Begin today to read the labels (in the Bible), heed the warnings and obey your spiritual instinct. Who knows . . . someday they will probably save your life.

★ ★ ★

Further Study: What warning label did you read today in the scripture? How does it apply now? With whom can you communicate what you've learned?

157

THE ART OF LISTENING

Listen to advice and accept instruction, and in the end you will be wise.
Proverbs 19:20

★ ★ ★

He had run with some of the roughest, toughest outlaws to ever show up on the Wild West scene. His area of expertise was his capability to crack the toughest bank vaults without ever laying a finger on them. You didn't read about him in your history books or see his story brought to life on the silver screen. His name was Tanner Watson, and he was blind at birth. He ran with Jesse James and "Wild Bill" Hickock. Their victims were towns like Tombstone, Abilene, Dodge City and Deadwood. They had to fight off Indians led by Sitting Bull and Crazy Horse along with cattle thieves out of the Mexican badlands south of Texas. The heyday of this historical cowboy lasted from 1867 to 1887, and life wasn't as glamorous or as romantically dangerous as it has been portrayed by the movies. Tanner survived those days to become the master of safe crackers. Because of his incredible ability to "listen" to the flaws in locks, he could pick them or figure out their combination in just a few turns of the dial. He would pull up a chair in front of the vault and have one of the outlaws spin the lock's dial until told to stop and write down the specific number they stopped on. This process was done day after day, bank after bank.

This Old West character had a gift that we can utilize in a little more positive, productive and much less dangerous way. The following techniques are a few ways in which you can increase your effectiveness in the art of listening:

Maintain eye contact.
Always sit or stand facing your partner.
Concentrate on what's being said.
Avoid distractions such as constant movement.
Use facial responses (nod) to show you're listening.
Ask relevant questions.
Re-state what your partner said to assure correct interpretation.

God has given each of us the capability of listening. Listening to someone translates into "you care." Be a collector of the tools for the art of listening.

★ ★ ★

Further Study: How well do you listen? What makes listening so hard? Why are there so few good listeners?

TRUTH AND CONSEQUENCES

This is what the Lord said, "Behold, I will raise up
evil against thee out of your own house."
2 Samuel 12:11

★ ★ ★

All we know of King David's beautiful daughter, Tamar, we learn from one chapter in 2 Samuel 13. This chapter, tough to read, is the beginning of the fulfillment of the prophet Nathan's strong words to David. David was reaping the consequences of adultery with Bathsheba and murder of her husband Uriah. David ignored warnings about marrying Maacha who bore two children, Absalom and Tamar. Amnon was the child of David and Ahinoam, and this dangerous combination is what set the explosive stage for a cover-up for rape. Amnon lusted for his half-sister Tamar. Amnon was a favorite of King David and an obvious heir to the throne. David granted an unusual request to Amnon to eat food at the hand of Tamar in his apartment. Amnon trapped her, then raped his naive half-sister and threw her out (2 Samuel 3:17) in disgrace. If he had been witnessed doing this act, he could have been tried for forcible rape and incest. With no witness, though, Amnon was free from persecution and was now trying to save face at the expense of his sister Tamar. Absalom found out about this event and, filled with hate, murdered Amnon in full view of his other brothers (2 Samuel 13:28-29), then fled to Geshur in exile for three years. Nathan's prophecy had been bitterly fulfilled: Amnon, the crown prince, was dead as a result of lack of morality; Absalom was dead as a result of rebellion and hate; Tamar was desolate in her brother's house (2 Samuel 13:20).

This sad story is a simple reminder of the true character of our Lord, which is . . . He is a God of love and mercy . . . judgment and consequences. God will bless you because you obey, or judge you with consequences because you didn't. Here, an innocent victim, Tamar, suffered disgrace and pain which were ultimately conceived by her father's (King David) disobedience. Our sins usually affect far more than just ourselves. What we do in disobedience today can and will affect our tomorrow. Trust and obey because . . . it is really the only way.

★ ★ ★

Further Study: Why does our culture tend to think in semesters, thinking that what I do in this semester doesn't affect the next one? How does disobedience carry over into the future? What does a life pursuing obedience reap?

159

THE REAL THING

Jesus Christ is the same yesterday and today, yes, forever.
Hebrews 13:8

★ ★ ★

When was the last time you were at your local Quik-Trip store and asked the attendant at the register for a Coke? You were probably presented, after the strange, clueless look, with a barrage of selections like nothing you've ever seen with the naked eye. You can get a Classic Coke, New Coke, Coke in a bottle, in a can, in a plastic bottle or liter, diet, sugar free, caffeine free, diet caffeine free, cherry . . . need I go on? Why does it take an act of Congress to make a decision that used to be a no brainer? It seems we have taken everything fun out of the "real thing" and made it into a close twin of pond water.

Isn't it a relief to know that our God doesn't change to suit the demands of others? What a nightmare, to think that Jesus would not be consistent in our future. What if He, just one day, woke up on the wrong side of a cloud in a bad mood and decided you weren't welcome in His family anymore? What if He decided we were saved by our works not grace, so we had to earn our way to those pearly gates? What if He decided He didn't love us and was tired of playing with what He created and dumped us like a hot potato? There is comfort in knowing that the Original is still the Original; the Classic is still the Classic, without any of the vital ingredients removed for the sake of keeping up with the fads of society. Read the verse above again   (I'll wait) . . . Jesus is the same forever and ever. Amen. This translates into having a Savior who follows through with what He started in perfecting us daily. Now, sit back, relax and ponder this some time today, and do yourself a favor, treat yourself to the "Real Thing."

★ ★ ★

Further Study: What would it be like if Jesus wasn't the same today as He was 2,000 years ago? How does consistency make you feel?

The Treasure

For where your treasure is, there will your heart be also.
Matthew 6:21

★ ★ ★

A farmer, soon before his death, wanted to tell his sons of a secret. He gathered the boys up and said, "Boys, I am soon to die of old age. I wanted to tell you of a hidden treasure that lies in the vineyard. Dig, and you will find it." Soon after, the father did pass away, and so the sons took a couple of shovels and other gardening tools and began to dig. They turned the soil in the vineyard over and over, yet found no buried treasure. What they did find was that because of all the digging and loosening of the soil, the vines produced abundantly and yielded a record breaking crop like none had ever seen before. The moral of the story is . . . there is no treasure without toil.

We all seem to be looking for that buried treasure throughout our lives. We want to live out those fantasies we see on all those Disney pirate movies. Little do we all realize that what we really treasure is what we talk of the most. In other words, all you have to do to find out what someone really treasures is listen to them for a while. We treasure various things like people, places, things, moments, memories, feelings, etc. God wants, and is literally jealous of our hearts, and desires us to treasure our relationship with Him. Don't forget though, just like the moral to the story, there will be no treasure without the accompanying labor. You don't ever just stumble upon your treasure like the movies portray; you'll have to inject a little time and toil. You're not limited to only one treasure chest either; just make sure that the most valued one is your relationship with your Savior in shining armor. I'm sure that when you uncover the hidden treasure chest and open it up, you'll find your heart there also.

★ ★ ★

Further Study: What do you treasure most in your life? What treasures have a way of coming between you and God? Why? What can you do to keep your heart in the right treasure chest? Why does work always shadow true fulfillment in our lives?

161

Sudden Death

There is a way that seems right to a man, but it ends in sudden death.
Proverbs 16:25

★ ★ ★

There are two arenas of conversation where you'll find the term, "sudden death." One is the sports arena, and the other is life. We love it in the first context and fear it in the other. It's not a subject fondly looked upon at a party or during dinner, yet it's destined to become reality in both circles. Death, or even the thought of it, runs a chill up one's spine. It's been said in a world of uncertainty, there are only two absolutes—death and taxes. The older you get the clearer this will become. The funny thing (sorry about my choice of words) about dying is that it really isn't the deciding time . . . it's just the final chapter. But once a person passes through those doors, we never hear from them what's on the other side. So, we must rely on the "faith factor."

My question to you is this . . . where are you going? Death is swift, sudden, sad, and very real. You will die and either spend eternity in torment and torture, or paradise and peace. The decisions and choices that you make today will affect your ultimate destiny. My suggestion to you, no matter how long you think you may live (no guarantees) or how comfortable you might become, is that you take a good hard look at yourself and see who is gonna' win in your sudden death. Side note: Don't think for a moment that you're gonna' take your worldly possessions with you to comfort you. Have you ever seen a U-Haul behind a hearse?

★ ★ ★

Further Study: If you were to die a sudden death today, where would your new residence be?

IT WILL FIND YOU OUT

And the Lord called to the man and said to him, "Where are you?" And he
(Adam) *said, "I heard the sound of You in the garden and I was afraid
because I was naked, so I hid." And He replied, "Who told you
that you were naked?"*
Genesis 3:9-11

* * *

It didn't take me long to break one of the Ten Commandments at the young age of 10, but I did it. I had just received one of those (what I thought at the time) manly items for my birthday . . . a cap gun. Listen up now because this assault weapon could make your ears ring like you'd just walked out of some rock concert. I mean, this was one of those heavy duty plastic jobs with the fake red barrel for visual effect. Only one small problem to overcome upon its arrival to me as a gift . . . no caps. That's right, my mom didn't quite get all the necessary items for me to reap havoc on my neighbors and sister (ha ha). The cost of one roll of caps was a $1.25, but I had no money in my piggy bank. The next day I accompanied my mom to Safeway (a grocery store) to pick up some milk and eggs. There I decided to permanently borrow from the toy rack a roll of caps. That's right, the old five finger discount, or you might just say stealing. I was successful in my first heist . . . until my mom asked me that fatal question. No, she didn't see me do it, or hear me shoot my gun (I may be dumb, but I'm not stupid). She simply asked me if I wanted to earn some allowance so I could buy some caps for my gun. My conscience was eating a hole in my stomach like battery acid on a T-shirt. I immediately broke down crying and confessed my offense in detail.

In the Garden of Eden, Adam and Eve knew they had done wrong and were guilty. It's the first time in the history of mankind we see that sin produces self-consciousness. God knew what they had done, but you read in Genesis 2:25 that they were naked and not ashamed until now. This is why God immediately knew they had done wrong by the simple fact they were hiding and ashamed to be naked. Sin causes us to look at ourselves and not others. It forces us (by guilt) to give ourselves away because we want to be found out to relieve the strain of guilt on our hearts. Take my word for it . . . your sin will find you out.

* * *

Further Study: How do you react when you're not right with God? What makes you self-conscience?

163

CASH MONEY

For the love of money is the root of all kinds of sin; some have wandered from the faith and pierced themselves with many griefs.
1 Timothy 6:10

★ ★ ★

You can't live with it, and you can't live without it. What is it? Cold, hard, cash money. There is nothing more consistently found in society today that causes marriages to malfunction, companies to crumble and societies to become stale, than money. I heard recently of a friend of mine who for the love of money lost a thriving business, his loving wife and now his blue-eyed, blonde-haired children. I spoke with this person on the phone and asked him a direct question, "Was it worth it?" You don't have to be a rocket scientist to figure out his answer . . . "No, no, no!" You can look throughout history and see that the dynamite that destroys so many circumstances is what is produced by the Department of Treasury daily. Guess what though? It's not the money itself that is the problem . . . it's the love of it. It's kind of like that cute toy poodle at your grandparents' house that looks harmless yet will bite the fire out of ya' when you touch it. Money can be a good thing if it's managed from a godly bank account. You can probably name several people (not many) that have lots of money yet keep it all in perspective. You'll probably also notice that those people who play with the poodle and don't get bitten are believers and givers.

Realize this, that money is the root of all types of evil if it's loved, and God gives and God takes away at His own free will. Don't get swindled by the theory that waits out there for you right after college graduation that tells you that "to have is happiness." That's one piece of advice that's not worth its weight in gold.

★ ★ ★

Further Study: How does the love of money affect you? How can you begin to de-program yourself of the thinking that money buys happiness?

UNWISE ADVICE

Wisdom comes from the abundance of wise (godly) *counsel.*
Proverbs 12:15

★ ★ ★

Nothing in our social system is given out as freely as advice. People will give it out for marriage, business deals, daily living, purchases and tastes, without even the slightest attempt at thinking ahead of their words. You will find out for the rest of your life, we live among a people who rarely seek the right kind of biblically-based counsel. There is a huge difference in advice and counsel. I'll make a gentleman's wager that at least two-thirds of the advice you receive today, and in the days to come, will have little regard for your best interest. If we made it a rule that everyone who gave advice must first give you a dollar (hit 'em where it hurts . . . in the pocketbook) every time they gave their airborne advice, things would be said less swiftly. scripture tells us to be "slow to speak and quick to listen" for a definite reason.

Look again at this nugget of scripture found in the book of Proverbs. Do you see that there are several words which are key in the context? First of all, make sure your counsel comes from more than one person, in fact several persons. Second, make sure it's wise (godly) counsel from sources who are walking with God on a daily basis. And lastly, make sure that it is not advice, but well thought out, pondered counsel which seeks to point you closer to your Savior. There are far too many of us who can find holes in the system and will seek counsel from the "rubber stamp" people. In other words, these fellows are the ones who give us the answer we want but not necessarily what is right or what we need.

Get yourself your own personal "board" of older individuals who think not as you do but are different, yet all follow the Savior sincerely. Use this group of folks to bounce off ideas, whims, thoughts or career moves. If a decision you're making affects your future, or others close to you, then give your board a call and ask them to think and pray about what the right answer is. Don't ask for a decision right then. This will take some pre-planning, but give them time to seek God's counsel first and then get back to you. Remember, advice is not what you're after. God-seeking counsel is.

★ ★ ★

Further Study: When was the last time you let someone else in on your decision making? What type counsel do you give?

YOUR MISSION

As for me and my house, we will serve the Lord.
Joshua 24:15

★ ★ ★

Every effective ministry I'm aware of has a statement of purpose in their material somewhere. A mission statement is a key ingredient in getting from point "A" to point "B" in a ministry. I am amazed how the organizations that don't have a mission statement make it, even for one year. The purpose of a mission statement is:

To direct.
To maintain a distinct purpose.
To hold accountable.
To assign a calling.
To deputize a task.

As you can plainly see . . . this way of attaining a specific goal isn't limited to Christian ministries. In fact–does your family have a mission statement? Why not? The first place we need these guidelines in place is with our families. What an awesome way to show to a community of friends and associates the direction your family is headed. Mission statements are useful tools for checking out other church and para-church organizations. They provide a window to the philosophy and theology of the group.

A mission statement should be a lot like an advertising slogan. Nike's "Just Do It" was a huge hit because it says so much in so few words. In the same way, a mission statement should make a point without being wordy. My personal guide is to say what needs saying in 20 words or less–that makes you think through what you want to communicate. Use direct, targeted words, not cliché or general terms. Make your mission statement a community of goals that can be used to direct your ship.

★ ★ ★

Further Study: Write out your own personal mission statement in 20 words or less. Sit down with your family after supper and write out a family mission statement, frame it and put it in your family room. Review this statement monthly and evaluate how you're doing personally and as a family.

WE'RE NOT JUST PLAYIN'

For the weapons of our warfare are not of the flesh, but divinely
powerful for the destruction of fortresses.
2 Corinthians 10:4

★ ★ ★

I guess you could classify me as an "outdoor fanatic," but I consider myself one who just loves to be out in the woods. One of my past motivations for getting out in the woods was hunting trips with my father, but now I find myself out there just to get out of chaos and watch animals on their turf. Living in Colorado offers ample opportunity for watching wildlife. It's just a short trip north to Estes Park where during the "mid-September Elk Bugle" a natural phenomenon takes place. The males (bulls) of the elk herds battle for dominance, going head-to-head, antler-to-antler, for breeding rights with the females (cows). The largest, heftiest, strongest antlered bull with the most endurance will win the battle of the hormones. The defeated bull leaves and the victorious bull licks its wounds and rests up for the next challenger. The lead "herd bull" will lose hundreds of pounds, tons of strength and suffer many wounds during the breeding season.

The ironic thing about this natural ritual is that the real battle is won during the summer when elk eat continually. The one that consumes the best diet for growing antlers and gaining weight will be the heavyweight champ of the fight in the fall. Those that eat inadequately sport weaker antlers that break in battle and obtain less bulk for the fall confrontations.

Satan will choose a season to attack. The question is whether we are prepared for the battle. Much depends on what we are doing now before the war begins. Enduring faith, strength and wisdom for the spiritual wars ahead are best developed before they're needed. We're not just playin' army . . . there's a war out there. Go get ready!

★ ★ ★

Further Study: In this spiritual war, will you walk away victorious or will you fall to defeat? Is this a serious battle? Do you think you're playin' army, or is it a war?

167

IRON ON IRON

Iron sharpens iron, so one man sharpens another.
Proverbs 27:17

★ ★ ★

Have you ever wondered why God didn't put each one of us on a planet of our own? I mean, hey, it's not like the universe in which we live doesn't have enough outer space places for us to live. Wouldn't it be cool to phone up a friend and tell him that your new address is 1124 East Venus, or Apartment 4 Jupiter Drive?

If you've never been to a blacksmith's metal working shop, you've missed out. The shop is full of scrap-iron piles, 75-pound anvils, coal burning furnace and lots of metal mallets. It's amazing to watch a true blacksmith mastering an old piece of black metal into a piece of art. When heated, the smith can force, bend, pound, torque and flatten any piece of iron into a useful tool. It's awesome to see that an iron hammer can contour an iron rod into a knife, a fireplace set or dinner bell. Two of the same materials can function for the same goal in the end.

No matter what you do or how you make your career, you will deal with people (iron). This world goes round because of common folks just like you and me. God placed us in the mortal madness for a distinct purpose and that is to be sharpened and shaped into a better person. Iron does sharpen iron. We, at times, would like to say, "Beam me up, Scotty" to escape this process, but we can't. You won't always see things the same way, have the same opinion, agree with a plan, like the same movies, date or marry the same type person, enjoy the same sports, read the same books, like the same foods, listen to the same music as others you come in contact with. God made each of us different and unique for a reason (praise God), and we should learn to appreciate and admonish our differences, not condemn them. So the next time you're about to blow a lid because someone doesn't see as you see, remember this, they are "no better, no worse, just different" (NBNWJD).

★ ★ ★

Further Study: What type people rub you the wrong way? Why? How can you learn to appreciate them?

Deadly Venom

And in their hearts they put God to the test
by asking according to their own desire.
Psalm 78:18

✦ ✦ ✦

On a cool, tranquil evening in the Georgia hill country, a congregation trickles into the "Church of the Lord Jesus Christ." Old parishioners chat, young couples juggle babies, and children play amid the pews. Cutting through the church-goers, three men stride quickly, carrying small wooden boxes, and place them near the pulpit. The service begins with a warning, "We have serpents up here, and there's death in their bite. If the Lord moves you to handle them, obey the Lord." The pastor pulls out a four-foot rattlesnake and a few sleek copperheads to wave around his head. The congregation screams, chants, convulses. This nonsense stems from misunderstanding the verse, "And these signs shall follow them that believe: In my name shall they cast out devils; speak with new tongues; take up serpents, and if they drink any deadly thing, it shall not hurt them" (Mark 16:17-18). The snake-handlers accept this verse out of context and believe if they have the faith, they won't get bitten. Suffering bites and deadly venom rarely discourage these people. Even though 75 to 100 people have died of bites, there are still those who follow this belief.

There are places of worship that allow a fallen person to receive clear thinking and good judgment. Gang, God will not be mocked or put to the test like a new hi-tech gadget. God is to be worshiped and left in a holy place. God is to be feared and respected as Jehovah. There were false prophets in Jesus' time and they are still around today. These false teachers use magic, illusion, lies, deceit, dictated conviction, control, physical force, and even sex to lure in their prey. James warned us not to be easily deceived. Faith in Jesus isn't avoiding a bite from a poisonous snake, it's "the assurance of things hoped for and the conviction of things not seen" (Hebrews 11:1).

✦ ✦ ✦

Further Study: How can you avoid falling victim to a false teacher? How can you avoid taking a verse out of context?

LIFE IN THE '90S

Be still and know that I am God.
Psalm 46:10

★ ★ ★

If you feel like you really are a person of the '90s and on the fast-track, then you probably see your life something like this:

Your life passes you by at 90 miles an hour.
You end up working 90 hours a week.
Your to-do list has 90 items on it.
You're on a 90 calorie a day diet because you're 90 pounds overweight.
You have at least 90 bills to pay each month.
Your bank account is $90 overdrawn.
The minimum payment on your credit card is $90 (and that's just interest).
You'll be paying off student loans for 90 more months.
You don't know where you'll get $90,000 to send your kids to college.
Your TV has 90 cable channels, and there's nothing good to watch.
You have 90 different activities to attend each week.
Your car just rolled over 90,000 miles.
You just answered the phone for the 90th time today.
The cheapest pair of tennis shoes you can find cost $90.
Life would be just grand if you only made $90,000 more a year.

Life in the '90s is definitely not all it's cracked up to be. It seems the faster you run, the further you lag behind, the days get shorter, while the list of things to do gets longer. Our lives get tangled in a web that can soon strangle us. We get so involved with our busy agenda that we lose sight of our purpose. God is not as concerned with what we do, as who we are in Christ. Take time away from the rat-race to be still and take quiet refuge with your Creator. You'll never cope with the agenda of the '90s until you tank-up with God for your fuel each day. Take a time-out and re-group.

★ ★ ★

Further Study: How busy are you? Are you too busy for God? When was the last time you were still? Do you meet with God in your stillness? When and where can you be still for 30 minutes a day to meet with your Savior in prayer and meditation?

FISHIN' HOLE

*And Jesus said to them, "Follow me, and I will make
you fishers of men"* (women too).
Mark 1:17

★ ★ ★

Before we begin, let me address you, ladies, before you turn this devotion off like a bad TV show. Please, (okay, pretty please with sugar on top) listen up because this verse applies to you as much as it does the guys. Have you ever been fishin', either on a lake, river, pond or ocean before? Well, if the answer is yes, then you will relate like an ol' relative. If not, maybe this will motivate you to try it.

Realize this first, that I grew up hunting, but never fishing, so I am definitely no Jimmy Houston (a Pro fisherman). I have done little that is as much fun to do with the whole family as landing a "lunker." We live close to a great trout lake and try to go as often as we can with the kids on weekends. There is nothing more exciting for a youngster than when the end of the pole takes a dip and begins to tug. Boy howdy, the kid's eyes light up as big as a Texas sunset, and the voice volume begins to go up at the expectation of catching a "Big One." Just the thought and anticipation of going to set the line will be enough, even if nothing is caught, to make a fishing outing a success.

I love the way that we can relate today with what happened yesterday in scripture. What would this world be like if we got as excited about "fishing for friends" as we do about "landing a lunker?" Notice that you don't have to be qualified to fish. God does that for you, and He will make you an angler for people's souls. Again, what a huge deal it is when God depends on you to follow Him, and in return you will catch others before they are caught by the evil one. Another important thing is that Satan always kills his catch, but God chooses the "catch and release" program. That release is called our freedom in Christ, something not many fine-finned fish can hope for.

★ ★ ★

Further Study: What pond are you fishin' in? What does your spiritual bait look like? Catchin' any?

171

A WEAK THINK

For as he thinks within himself, so he is.
Proverbs 23:7

★ ★ ★

Years ago I went along with a handful of fellow believers on a mission trip to Trinidad. Now, hear me out, I couldn't even spell it, much less feel spiritual enough to do such a trip-but I went anyway. To give you a run down of this Third World country is a sad story. Dirt poor, used and abused by the oil industry, no stable government in place, apathy running rampant, immorality evident and directions to nowhere. Our mission was to go door to door to every house on the island and personally share Jesus with a population whose religious melting pot included Hindus, Muslims and a few Rastifarians for flavor. While sharing with a gas station attendant for about 30 minutes, I looked over the register counter to see a sign that read, "The brain is only as strong as its weakest think." What a fact of scriptural truth, yet a catchy play on the original, "the chain is only as strong as its weakest link."

If you think for a moment, you'll realize all it took for adultery, murder, theft, gossip, lying, disobedience, rebellion, lust, greed, envy and a long, long list was a weak think moment. What's that? That is a time when you weren't in tune with God and you followed the old nature path. It's the second you gave up hope for harmony, purity for passion or contentment for compromise. Realize that you are gonna' have those weak moments, you will lose a few battles (you're saved, not perfect), but you don't have to lose the war. We are overcomers!

★ ★ ★

Further Study: When was the last "weak think" moment you had? How can you avoid it next time? What prevents those moments in your life?

ReRuns

As far as the east is from the west, so far has God thrown away our sins from us.   Psalm 103:12

★ ★ ★

They're back! What's back? Old reruns (and they're great)! The Andy Griffith Show, Flipper, Superman (black and white version), Bonanza, The Adams Family, The Brady Bunch, The Partridge Family, Leave It To   Beaver . . . you betcha', and they're worth bringing back from the sitcom cemetery to live again. Have you had the fortune, and I do mean fortune, of tuning in your tube to one of these vintage shows? The networks have begun to air these oldies but goodies on weekday afternoons. Some shows are in black and white, the clothes worn are so outdated they're back in style, and the hair-do's are real doosers. The plots are simple, the pace is slow, the sets simple, the humor tired and the language clean. Do yourself a favor and feast your fancy on one of these re-runs soon, soon, very soon. They're so bad, they're good. I suppose the thinking behind the network big shots' decision is to appeal to those older generations who grew up watching these shows. To be honest, it's not a bad way of getting viewers to watch a little tube in their busy daily schedules. Even though the targeted audience may be a little older and grayer, they still have a memory that works.

I'm glad that God doesn't like to watch old re-runs of us and our mess-ups. We have a Creator that has all the capability (like a computer) and technology (like a laboratory) and storage space to retain the films of us falling short in our Christian walks. God could very easily air our sins back to us at judgment day. He could keep a little list of the times we chose our way and not His. He could point out just how big of a scab we all are and make us feel like an old shoe. He could keep the score in this game, and I bet we'd see we lose by a lot. Guess what? He doesn't! He says that after we confess and repent of them, He takes all our bloopers and throws them so far that even man can't measure the distance. Correct me if I'm wrong here, but that's one heck of a throw, and I'm glad. heaven doesn't show re-runs! And God seems to have a bad memory, too!

★ ★ ★

Further Study: How far is east from west? When does God throw our sins away? Do you have some you need chucked? What does this gift do for your relationship with Him?

FROG IN THE KETTLE

He who separates himself seeks his own desire,
he quarrels against the sound of wisdom.
Proverbs 18:1

★ ★ ★

We've all heard the analogy about the frog in the kettle. The idea behind this is that when you put a frog in lukewarm water and slowly heat it up to a boil, he obviously will become frog soup. Not only that, he will never even realize the temperature is rising.

You know, the same thing can happen to us if we are not careful. That Proverb reminds us that whenever we separate ourselves from the Word of God, we argue against what we know is right from the Word of God.

Psalm 119:9 reminds us that a man keeps his way pure by keeping it according to God's Word, not worldly ways. We must remain constantly (daily) in the Word. It is the only sure thing in a changing world. The frog in the kettle analogy can happen to anyone, at any age. None of us are above being pulled away slowly by the world. Satan is very cunning in how he lures each of us in his own way. If we are not saturated in the Word, we become very easy victims of his tactics.

The Word of God is not a bunch of outdated, unrelated fiction stories about people who never were. It is exactly what it says it is . . . The Word of God.

★ ★ ★

Further Study: When have you seen yourself make a bad decision because you have not spent time in the Word? Why is it so hard for us to remain consistent in God's Word? How can we become like Jesus if we don't know what He is about or what He says?

174

OUR TIMES

Men who understood the times with knowledge of what they should do.
1 Chronicles 12:32

✫ ✫ ✫

What if you went into a final exam without studying or challenged a team without scouting them first? We live in an information rich country which prides itself on being there when the action happens. News stations and major networks spend millions of dollars on equipment designed to allow live broadcasts from random locations. If you want to find out what has happened in our world, country or cities in the last 10 minutes, all you need is a remote or 25 cents for a paper. We have the capability (or technology) to be on top of the trends and times in a matter of minutes. The warning is that we can be fed the wrong perspective on the wrong story. In other words, our madness of media is a melting pot for a secular humanistic view. Our liberal media can spoon feed us, from behind the desk of the nightly news, a method of thinking and viewing certain situations. We, as a nation, saw the power of the media during the presidential race between George Bush and Bill Clinton.

You have a responsibility and a duty to keep up with what's going on around you. I like to say, "keeping your finger on the pulse of the times." You can do this by watching the news, reading the papers, listening to tapes and reading books. Make sure these sources are reliable and conservative in nature. Don't just say this world is going downhill fast without making an effort to re-direct its course to the Cross. We, as Christians, are not of the world, yet we do live in the world by Divine design. Understanding the times of our world will help us direct our lives. We must view the news with a critical eye and acknowledge it's run mostly by secular people who have not the knowledge of Christ. Make sure you spend more time studying the original (Bible) and not the counterfeit. Doing this allows you to tell what is true and what is false.

✫ ✫ ✫

Further Study: How much do you understand the times in which we live? How can you prevent being fed slanted liberal news? What one area will you choose to do something about?

WHATEVER, DUDE

Finally, brethren, whatever is true, honorable, right, pure, lovely,
of good repute, if there is any excellence and if anything
worthy of praise, let your mind dwell on these things.
Philippians 4:8

★ ★ ★

It's a pretty uncommon sight for a school, office or now even a home to be without a computer. The Age of Aquarius has evolved into the age of technology. Schools are training our youth to use computers from kindergarten up. The computer has brought to the table organization, memory, data processing and graphics like never before. You would think this conglomeration of wires, plastics and micro chips had a mind of its own. Realize this, a computer is a tool, and only as smart as its programmer. *Excel, Pagemaker* and *ClarisWorks* weren't programmed by a computer named Bob. Millions of dollars are being made by professional programmers coming up with developing programs for business and personal computers. A computer takes the input, stores it, performs calculations or processes on it, then spits it back up as output when recalled (how's that for simplicity?).

Your mind is a super computer. When used properly, it is a tremendous tool that can recall details from years past, visualize scenes from TV shows and old movies, trigger emotions, control every muscle movement, distinguish between two means and create new ideas. Whether you realize it or not, whatever you see and listen to (input), goes directly into your mind for processing. Every bed scene on TV, every curse word on the silver screen, every lyric at a concert, every word blurted out of the radio. You are being programmed by someone and its root is either in heaven or hell. Your mind is like a sponge, your eyes like a camera, catching every move and wiping up every worldly spill. Be careful and downright picky about what you watch, listen to and who you follow. Set your mind on things above and not below. Be your own censor and screen the bad from your mind. Remember, what you are is connected to what you think.

★ ★ ★

Further Study: How careful are you with your mind? Do you screen what goes in or is it an open door policy?

FOLLOWING IN MY FATHER'S PAW PRINTS

Many are the plans (future) *in a man's heart, but the
counsel of the Lord will stand.*
Proverbs 19:21

★ ★ ★

From the magnificent musical opening and breath-taking African vistas, to the rip-roaring, (pun . . . get it?), emotionally charged climax, *The Lion King* movie reigns as animation's supreme champion. Set in the majestic beauty of the Serengeti, Disney's epic tells the heart-warming story of the love between a proud lion ruler, Mufasa, and his young son, Simba–a curious cub who "just can't wait to be king." Out from the darkness crawls Simba's jealous Uncle Scar and his hyena hitmen. Their scheming for the throne leads to Mufasa's tragic death, and Simba's exile from the kingdom he should rightfully rule. Befriended by the warmhearted warthog, Pumbaa and his maniac friend, Timon, Simba forgets his responsibilities and adopts the carefree lifestyle of "Hakuna Matata" (means: don't worry). Rafiki, the wise and mysterious baboon, helps Simba reclaim his territory and eventually his position as King, just like his father.

This devotion is targeted mainly at the male species who roam this jungle of society searching for prey . . . the future. This is one devotion I feel I am qualified (somewhat) to write. I grew up with a huge desire to follow in my father's footsteps (paw prints). Males often don't realize until later on in life what an influence their fathers can have on them. God (our true Father) has a specific, hand-picked, custom designed plan for our lives and future. There is nothing wrong with wanting to do as your dad, but don't be disappointed (or surprised) if God's way points another direction. Some reading this may very well take up where their dad left off . . . but remember, no one is a failure if God leads them to a different destination. Always remember to enjoy and learn along life's journey until coming face-to-face with our Savior in eternity. Keep on prowling!

★ ★ ★

Further Study: What does (did) your father do for a living? Do you see yourself following his footsteps? Why or why not? What if God's plans are different than your father's? Is that okay? Are you sure?

ACTING CHILDISH

Unless you become like little children, you won't enter the kingdom of heaven.
Matthew 18:3

★ ★ ★

It's amazing to me as a parent how we think we will handle our kids differently than our parents handled us. We find ourselves reminding our kids: share, play fair, don't hit, pick up after yourself, if you don't have anything nice to say—don't say anything, don't take things that aren't yours, watch for traffic, say you're sorry, stick together and hold hands. Instructions received from our parents are for our best interest. I find myself giving out orders like a general because I desire my children to steer clear of the hazards of life. I'm not a big rule person, but I have realized that the rules I initiate in my household are motivated by love for my kids, not because I dig laying down the law.

Scripture is full of boundaries and guidelines to heed for our own good. My boys must have faith that their father knows what's best for his kiddos, and desires the best for their well-being. God has the same perspective as human parents, but we need faith in Him as our Creator to understand. God warns us in His word to flee sexual immorality, love our neighbor, be thankful, never steal or lie, live an unstained life and so on. Why? Because He wants to be a Hitler god? Not! Because He loves to write rules? No way! Because He is crazy in love with us as His own children? You bet! Heed the warning of Jesus Himself. If you don't have that child-like faith (faith that will jump from anywhere, any height, into your father's arms because you know he won't drop you), you won't inherit a spot in that heavenly hotel. Grow up and be a child. What??

★ ★ ★

Further Study: Are you a child of God? Do you obey your Father in heaven? Did you (or do you) obey your parents' standards?

178

ABRASIVNESS

What is desirable in a man is his kindness.
Proverbs 19:22

★ ★ ★

Gentleness is a word not often used in circles of conversation these days. I recall a story from April 19, 1992, about former U.S. Senator John Tower of Texas and 22 others. The *Chicago Tribune* headline read, "Gear Blamed in Crash That Killed Senator." A stripped gear in the propeller controls of a commuter plane caused the plane to take a nose-dive into the Georgia woods. A specific gear that adjusted the pitch of the left engine's propellers was slowly worn down by an opposing part with a harder titanium coating, the National Transportation Safety Board reported. It acted like a file and over an extended time period, wore down the teeth that controlled the propeller. Once the teeth were sheared off, the mechanism was not able to continue working.

After reading this article, the thought that we can be a hard material that wears other weaker working materials (people) out hit me like a ton of bricks. Like the titanium-coated gear wore away the softer gear engaged to it, so one abrasive, unkind friend can wear away the spirit of another. To be kind to someone else is to have the spirit of God thriving (living actively) in your life. Don't be a titanium person who goes throughout life wearing down others by abrasive words and actions. Gentleness is a great way to attract friends and bond relationships that will last a lifetime. Abrasion kills others and sends friends into a nosedive of despair.

★ ★ ★

Further Study: Would anyone describe you as kind? Why not? Are you an abrasive friend that wears down others? How can you practice kindness in your relationship?

179

A NEW WAY OF THINKING

No one puts new wine into old wineskins; otherwise, the
new wine will burst the skins and it will be spilled out,
and the skins will ruin. But new wine must be put
into new wineskins and both are preserved.
Luke 5:37-38

★ ★ ★

Have you ever run across one of those passages of scripture that seemed to have applied to you as much as fleas on a dog? That's right, it just doesn't seem to fit your life, nor does it look like it ever will. For years I seemed to have stumbled over this verse in the gospel of Luke like a big pair of shoes in a dark hallway and never quite clued in to its real meaning. What this verse is saying, simply stated in modern terminology, is to keep the standards, yet apply them and use them more creatively. This whole devotional book is meant to come alive in the present. If you're gonna' bore someone, don't bore them with the Bible. It's key that we don't water down the richness of scripture, yet learn new ways and challenge ourselves daily on how we can creatively make God's word more exciting in a stagnant society. You can do things a new, exciting, different way without compromising your commitment to Christ. How about it . . . take a moment today to sit back and let those creative juices flow. After all, didn't Jesus do this same thing when His life and teachings could not be contained within the old rigid system of the Mosaic Law? Wasn't He the one who first put the new covenant (new wine) into a new generation during His days? Come on gang, let's show this ol' world just how fashionable our faith can really be.

★ ★ ★

Further Study: When was the last time you used a recent event or illustration to prove a point out of past scripture? Try it . . . it's eye opening!

WHO BROKE THE BABY?

You shall not murder.
Exodus 20:13

★ ★ ★

Well, well, let me think a minute . . . (that's long enough). Where, oh where have we seen or heard this little four-word phrase before? I know! I know! It was when Moses scaled down that mountain called Sinai after his meeting with God-In-Person. He was carrying those tablets with the "Ten Suggestions" on them, right? Absolutely wrong, Pickle Lips! If your Bible reads the same as mine, I do believe they were called the "Ten Commandments," not suggestions. Herein lies the problem that we face today . . . folks don't respect, adhere, listen to, abide by, or follow these commandments, or worse yet, can't even identify these 10 phrases of protection! I won't bore you with mind bloating statistics on our subject of discussion today–abortion. Help me out; clue me in; beam me up; do whatever tickles your fancy, but tell me how people get off on the idea that we have a "pro-choice" to eliminate human life? How and where did we develop the standard that if life inconveniences us, we play God and choose someone else's destiny? I mean, hey, the next time someone pulls out in front of you while you're driving, just pull out your trusty six-shootin' handgun and kill 'em! (Sound absurd? It is, but so is abortion.)

Forgive me for being on my soapbox, but reader (you!), clue in and realize we are going "to hell in a hand basket" as a society. God commands us not to kill anyone, no how, no way, no one. Children are a gift from God no matter how they are conceived. I have a question. Is God all knowing? Does He know who is pregnant now (even if they don't) and who will be pregnant in their lifetime? Then why, even if someone becomes pregnant out of wedlock, do we think we, as a civilized (questionable) society, can choose someone else's destiny? Come on people, the choice is and always will be God's. Bombing clinics and killing doctors is not the solution to this problem–it's that people need a Savior, and you need to tell them about yours. The right choice is God's choice.

★ ★ ★

Further Study: Can you write down all Ten Commandments? Why do we have these guidelines? Will you memorize and live by them?

LASER GUIDED PRAYER

I urge then, first of all, that requests, prayers, intercession
and thanksgiving be made for everyone.
1 Timothy 2:1

★ ★ ★

During Operation Desert Storm, the Iraqi war machine (the tank) was overwhelmed by the Coalition Force's ability to strike strategic targets with never-before-seen accuracy. Unknown to the Iraqis, the Allied Supreme Command dropped "Special Operations Force" (SOF) units deep behind enemy lines. These men provided bombing coordinates for military targets and first-hand reports on the effectiveness of subsequent bombing missions by the U.S. Air Force. To avoid unintended targets, pinpoint bombing was often required. A soldier from an SOF unit, standing on the ground, would request an aircraft high overhead to drop a laser-guided missile. Using a hand-held laser, the soldier would point at the target. The missile would lock on the target for a direct hit.

In much the same way, the prayers of Christian focus are often general in intent. Our prayers and conversations with God should target specific needs and petitions. A good way to pray is:

1. Praise God for who He is.
2. Confess sins.
3. Petition for needs of others.
4. Thank Him for answers which come as yes, no, or wait.

Take time out of each day to commune with God. Pray specifically for things you would like to see Him take over. Pray to Him like you would reveal needs and concerns with your best friend. Prayer is what we need to do before we do anything. Prayer and God's Word are the only two offensive weapons we have as Christians. Use them wisely, and you will win this spiritual war.

★ ★ ★

Further Study: Spend the next 15 minutes praying.

SAY IT ISN'T SO

And Simon answered and said, "Master, we worked (fished) hard all night
and caught nothing, but because you (Jesus) say so, I will let down my nets."
Luke 5:5

✫ ✫ ✫

This is one of those "gold nuggets" of scripture that, after you read it, causes tons of lessons and practical applications to flood from the page. Will you do yourself a favor and read Luke 5:1-11?

I am sitting on my front porch in Castle Rock, Colorado, after supper on a cool August evening, watching a rainstorm roll over the Rockies, reading the same passage of scripture you just read. If you don't mind, I'd like to share a few thoughts, then you as a family do the same around the supper table. The scene sets itself up perfectly as the three amigos Peter, James and John are out all night fishing. Obviously they aren't new at this, nor is the water they are fishing foreign uncharted waters. Jesus is overrun by a crowd, so He takes His podium into a boat and preaches off shore. After He's done, he offers a bit of advice to Peter, who takes it and makes the catch of all catches. Peter catches so many fish that his fishing boat begins to take on water (sink), and so does James and John's boat.

Now, what struck me was this . . . Jesus was a carpenter, these three were fisherman, yet they listened and didn't smart off at Jesus' request to go back where they just came from (unsuccessfully) and try it again. None of the three were disciples yet, but they still obeyed and were blessed. After Peter "saw," he was humbled at the feet of Jesus and worshiped Him along with his comrades. Jesus told them not to fear; from now on they would-n't catch fish, but men (unsaved folks). And finally, they left all they owned (boat, nets, family, possessions, boat-load of fish, which meant cash money) and followed Him as disciples of Christ. WOW! What a story of obedience, humility, courage, fear, priorities, compassion and love. Now it's your turn . . . what are the lessons you got out of it? Go ahead and say it isn't so.

✫ ✫ ✫

Further Study: What one "nugget" did you get out of this message of scripture you can apply today? Will you do it?

A CHEERFUL GIVER

Let each one do just as he has purposed in his heart, not grudgingly
or under compulsion; for God loves a cheerful giver.
2 Corinthians 9:7

★ ★ ★

There tells a story of a wealthy man who lived in Scotland years ago. He had outlived all of his family and was recently diagnosed with a terminal illness that would allow him only a few months to live. He had been successful in about every business deal he had been involved with and was looked upon by the locals in high esteem. During the final chapter of his life he wanted to know what it was like to live as a beggar on the streets, scurrying for food like a street rat. One day he was digging through a pile of rubbish for a morsel of food when a poor young boy came up to join in the search. After a few minutes the boy, being a pro, found half a loaf of stale bread, and the wealthy man found none. The boy, with excitement of the find, jumped for joy and began to devour the bread. All of a sudden, he noticed the wealthy man (disguised as a beggar) had no food, so he gave him the half loaf and walked away. The man, heartfelt at what had just taken place, ran after the boy to say thanks. He asked the boy, "Why did you give me your only meal this week?" to which the poor boy replied, "To give is to get." The man, amazed at the boy's answer and heart, decided to give him his entire inheritance of wealth.

We live in a "me first" world where our national motto should be "looking out for number one" (and that's self). What a joy it is to have the privilege of giving to someone in need. In the story of the widow's mite, you see a great example of not only giving of a mite (last penny), but also giving with a cheerful heart. Giving comes from the heart, not the pocketbook. Giving doesn't necessarily have to be money; it could be a listening ear, service or time. God loves a joyful giver who's not as concerned with the 10 percent tithe issue as He is the attitude in which you give. What a testimony you will be to simply meet someone's need by giving. Who knows, God has His ways of rewarding you far better than you'll ever know from a savings account. Remember, to get, you've got to give it up.

★ ★ ★

Further Study: When was the last time you gave? Who could you give to today? What does Jesus say in His word about giving? (Look it up.)

CHURCH CHOOSING

*Realize this, in the last days, difficult times will come. For men will become
lovers of self, money, boastful, arrogant, disobedient to parents, ungrateful,
unholy, unloving, gossips, brutal, haters of good, conceited, lovers of pleasure
rather than lovers of God; holding to a form of godliness although
they have denied its power; avoid such men as those.*
2 Timothy 3:2-5

★ ★ ★

For years I thought that this verse was aimed at communicating the
details of a fallen world headed for hell in a hand basket. It seems to give
the specifics of what this society will be looking like prior to the return of
the Creator. Guess what? There are two ways to look at something . . . my
way and the right way. It just so happens that Paul is describing what the
Church is going to look like with all its splendor in the last days. Don't
hang up on me yet and mishear what I'm saying. I am an avid church
member and a firm believer in the body of Christ meeting weekly. I'm not
big on giant steeples, ornate pews and lofty budgets being our only definition of a church, but I do believe the Church is the bride of Christ. Take
a moment to read this scripture again . . . slowly.

Beware of a church and a teacher (pastor or priest) who don't preach
the truth and live it out in their own lives. Heed the warnings Paul gives
Timothy in these verses of validity: there will be churches that are not
what God intended them to be. How do you know if a church is for real?
What sort of check-list can be used to test its spiritual substance? A legitimate church 1) takes God and the Bible seriously, believes it is the inher-
ent word, teaches about Jesus' deity, servanthood, humility, faith, purity,
creation, agape love, discipleship, heaven and hell, and doesn't water down
or misuse scripture, 2) looks hard at what God has wrapped up in you; has
some expectations of you and how your unique contributions can be better used in the body of Christ; helps you to realize your importance in the
family, 3) is an equipping church; provides its congregation with tools to
live; pastoral staff sees itself as a coaching staff; equips you to do the work
of the ministry. Once you've found a church that qualifies, pour not only
your heart into it, but your actions too . . . it's well worth the effort.

★ ★ ★

Further Study: What should a godly church look and act like? Do a check-
list on your   church . . . how does it come out?

185

GREATNESS

Know therefore that the Lord your God is God; He is the faithful God, keeping
His covenant of love to a thousand generations of those
who love Him and keep His commands.
Deuteronomy 7:9

★ ★ ★

Gladys Aylward, a missionary to China more than 50 years ago, was forced to flee when the Japanese invaded Yangcheng. She was so dedicated to her cause she just couldn't leave her work behind. With only one assistant, she led more than 100 orphans over the mountains toward free China. In their book, *The Hidden Price of Greatness*, Ray Besson and Ranelda Hunsicker tell what happened:

During Gladys's harrowing journey out of a war-torn Yangcheng . . . she grappled with despair as never before. After passing a sleepless night, she faced the morning with no hope of reaching safety. A 13-year old girl in the group reminded her of their much-loved story of Moses and the Israelites crossing the Red Sea.

"But I am not Moses," Gladys cried in desperation.

"Of course you aren't," the little girl replied, "but Jehovah is still God!" The purpose of sharing this unique story is to illustrate a point which holds true some 50 years later. When Gladys and the orphans made it through to safety, they proved once again that no matter how inadequate we feel (don't let your feelings become facts), God is still God, and we can trust in Him in every circumstance. I recall a friend telling me early in my life, "God doesn't call the qualified, He qualifies the called." scripture logs a multitude of stories (true ones) that reveal just how involved God our Father is in each of our lives. You will be confronted with odds that seem overwhelming at a glance, but are peanuts to God. The same God of the Old Testament is still active and working today in lives and situations to provide a way to victory if we only trust Him. You don't have to "have it all together" or "be perfect" for God to use you in a situation that glorifies Him. God is in the business of pulling off miracles against all odds.

★ ★ ★

Further Study: How big is God? Why is God so interested in you and your life that He even knows the number of hairs on your head? What does God ask from you to pull off a miracle? How deep is your faith and strong is your trust in Him? What could you do today to strengthen them?